Thinking in Common

Community in the Global Era

PETER LANG

Bruxelles · Bern · Berlin · New York · Oxford · Wien

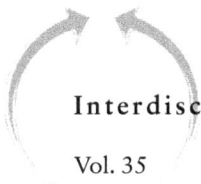

Interdisciplinary and Plurilingual Work

Vol. 35

In collaboration with the CRPM (Centre de Recherches Pluridisciplinaires Multilingues) of the University of Paris Nanterre, the "Travaux Interdisciplinaires et Plurilingues" series aims to promote interdisciplinary and plurilingual research. It welcomes works which contribute to the understanding of cultural, national and transnational imaginaries, in their historical, political, translational and media dimensions.

Series edited by
Dorothée Cailleux, Lucia Quaquarelli and Licia Reggiani

Scientific board
Sylvie Aprile, *Université Paris Nanterre*
Pascale Cohen-Avenel, *Université Paris Nanterre*
Michael Cronin, *Trinity College Dublin*
Rainier Grutman, *Université d'Ottawa*
Marina Guglielmi, *Università di Cagliari*
Brigitte Krulic, *Université Paris Nanterre*
Rita Monticelli, *Università di Bologna*
Jean Robert Raviot, *Université Paris Nanterre*
Lawrence Venuti, *Temple University*
Eric Vial, *Université de Cergy-Pontoise*
Yoan Vilain, *Humboldt Universität Berlin*
Dirk Weissmann, Université Toulouse Jean Jaurès

PETER LANG
Bruxelles • Bern • Berlin • New York • Oxford • Wien

Pascale Cohen-Avenel,
Lucia Quaquarelli (eds.)

Thinking in Common

Community in the Global Era

PETER LANG

Bruxelles · Bern · Berlin · New York · Oxford · Wien

Bibliographic Information published by the Deutsche Nationalbibliothek The Deutsche Nationalbibliothek lists this publication in the Deutsche National-bibliografie; detailed bibliographic data is available online at http://dnb.d-nb.de.

The publication of this book was made possible by the generous financial support of the Université Paris Lumières.

UPL
UNIVERSITÉ
PARIS LUMIÈRES

ISSN 1663-9367
ISBN 978-2-8076-1412-3
ePUB 978-2-8076-1414-7
D/2021/5678/57

DOI 10.3726/b18765
ePDF 978-2-8076-1413-0

© P.I.E. PETER LANG s.a.
Éditions scientifiques internationales
Bruxelles, 2022
1 avenue Maurice, B-1050 Bruxelles, Belgique
www.peterlang.com ; brussels@peterlang.com

This publication has been peer reviewed.

Summary

Producing "the common"

Pascale Cohen-Avenel, Lucia Quaquarelli

Ou bien la masculinité, la féminité, la nation, les frontières, les démarcations territoriales et linguistiques l'emportent sur l'infinitude des séries possibles de relations établies et à établir, ou bien nous fabriquons ensemble l'enthousiasme expérimental capable de soutenir un processus constituant perpétuellement ouvert.

Paul B. Preciado, 2019

Today, the notion of "globalisation" is particularly difficult to wield. Although it seems to cover economic, political, social and cultural phenomena that mark and define our era and our relationship to the world, it is never, as Appadurai wrote, "a total project", that takes hold "of all geographies with the same force" (2013: 88). The circulation of men and women, like those of goods, ideas and imaginings, which is supposedly free (and free-market) as well as transnational, takes place following the pattern of a very centralised hierarchical organisation which reactivates old hegemonic dynamics, reproducing a concrete and symbolic system of subordination and exploitation. In short, it takes the shape of an unequal, unfair (and often violent), selective and differential social construction that denies any possibility of a unitary, egalitarian and free world citizenry. What is at stake is not only the relation between local and global, or between homogenisation and heterogenisation – from which we have become used to situating, problematising and reading globalised and globalising practices and flows; what is at stake is also the more general epistemic question that prefigures, allows and guarantees the very existence of these flows and these practices in a framework in which the world is not the whole world where not all men and women enjoy the same rights "of passage", or the same possibilities of appropriation, of sharing and of re-semantising the common space.

If "every social community, reproduced by the functioning of institutions, is imaginary" (Balibar, Wallerstein 1997: 127), if it is the result of a largely fictional configuration, legitimised by the projection of individual existence on the image of a collective narrative – the one which, for example, gave birth and authority to the Nation-State, to the Empire-State –, what is the narrative underpinning the "World-State" that allows it to exist, to function and exercise its violence, both real and symbolic? Likewise, which other narratives could be possible? Which other narratives escape from the "striature" (Mezzadra 2008: 13), from the interstices of the global space?

It is on the basis of these statements and questions that a group of researchers from the Centre de Recherches Pluridisciplinaires Multilingues from Université Paris Nanterre in collaboration with the Institut Français de Géopolitique has been working since 2018 on the "Tournant global" (Caillé, Dufoix 2013) to question discursive, normative and political instances starting from a cross-disciplinary approach that aims to be both an opportunity to diversify analytical tools and references and an exercise in decentralising scientific thought.

The group publication that these few lines attempt to introduce presents the initial results of research that questions globalisation in terms of its capacity to generate communities beyond political and geographical borders, around a *common*, that, after the "conflagration" (Blanchot 1984) of the meaning of community must be rethought beyond, or even upstream of, any hegemonic logic of unification, of any process of reducing differences to one (single) common. It must, in short, rewrite relations between individual and universal whose antinomy, wrote Agamben once and for all, "ha la sua origine nel linguaggio" (Agamben 2001: 18) and whose danger spans, marks and wounds our history.

Thus, how in a globalised space – at once trans-national, post-national, supra-national and infra-global –, can *another common* emerge, which, instead of ignoring, or at worst, eliminating all individual otherness, enhances plurality and initiative in a federating manner? Grounded in which modalities and which processes does this common engender communities or not? How is the common expressed (constructed, spoken, sold) on a global scale? Can globalisation be envisaged as a mesh of narratives of another common? Can communities spring from this common?

This publication presents and questions some of these factories of the common in order to seize the opportunity, perhaps, to see and think through another relation to others, another modality of living together, that is, living and being, because the very nature of being is undoubtedly "being-with" (Nancy 1996: 78). A life, writes Judith Butler "cannot be a life without others". A life can only be lived with others for the *critical conditions* of democratic life to come together and, Butler continues, for us to respond to the emergencies of our times with another "form of thinking and acting" (2016: 270). A form of thinking that, to be contemporary, has to adhere to its era "whilst maintaining a distance" (Agamben 2008: 11), that is, practicing a temporal, spatial and semantic "de-phasing" capable of establishing "epistemic disobedience" (Mignolo 2015) within which the imbrications between spatiality, modernity and power are visible, taken into account and "decolonised".

It seems necessary then, as Stéphane Dufoix has done in the opening of this book, to rethink globalisation above all from a "geoepistemic" approach that can depotentiate its supposed universality – in revealing it as unfounded, illusory, instrumentalised and violent – by a decentred, decolonised approach that refuses to read the history of Northern thought as the "history of thought in general".

This epistemic approach thus allows globalisation to be apprehended as a multi-faceted process from which new forms of post-national communities emerge that are more or less stable, more or less numerous, in line with very diverse modalities that, not only can be grounded in other bases than the common but may also generate new interactions between humans as well as between humans and non-humans. This line of thought imposes itself due to the urgency of the Anthropocene's environmental crisis but also due to an all-too-frequent acceptation of a purely economic rationale of deregulated worldwide competition. This perspective is the context for articles by Radu Cinpoes on the analysis of Margaret Archer's categorises confronted with Greta Thunberg's *School strike for Climate* movement, by Rémi Astruc on the notion of community in Bruno Latour's ANT Theory, by Fabienne Martin on the smart-city on Miyako Island as well as Antonin Chambon's on Jewish mysticism.

As Rémi Astruc writes, "the new weight of ecological and environmental crisis in our lives" heavily criticised by Latour (2015) "reveals more bluntly than ever before the crisis of occidental modernity (Latour 1991)". Yet it also obliges us, more than ever before, to constitute communities to counter this situation. In confronting the categories elaborated by Archer based on the concepts of morphogenesis and meta-reflexitivity with the *School strike for Climate* movement created in 2018 by Greta Thunberg Radu Cinpoes shows the modalities by which new communities generated by cyberspace and an awareness of the world environmental crisis can liberate a possible space for intervention on the forces of resistance and inaction of political, social, cultural or economic agencies and structures (morphostasis) on a global scale. Centred on the 21st century, this study allows us to question the emergence of specific forms of reflexivity and interactions enabled by new forms of web 2.0 telecommunications on three different levels: micro (that of the individual, specifically Greta Thunberg), macro (the social order) and intermediate (that of social networks).

The smart-city Miyako can be considered as one of these attempts to overturn structural routine through a connected community by imposing a real action that can reverse the self-destructive forward march of the comfort society based on industry. Fairly close to the theoretical postulate of Latour's ANT, the smart city sees the world as a network in which Myako Island would be both a module and an incarnation rich in contradictions that reveals the cultural and technological issues raised by this new form of community. Although the smart city aims to resolve the environmental crisis on a global scale, the solution it proposes rests entirely on the technology that is responsible for the environmental crisis in the first place. Its objective, as well as the possibility of reducing the environmental impact of human activity is also to maintain, or even improve, the level of comfort guaranteed by industrialisation. Furthermore, the interconnection of all the factors on a global scale tends to ignore all other scales, particularly the local. By placing all actors on the same – uniquely planetary – level, the smart city risks erasing a sense of local identity, considered as illegitimate and inefficient, wiping out in one stroke the glocal dimension, which is nonetheless one of globalisation's key mechanisms (Robertson 1994). The smart city of Miyako can thus be considered as the paroxysm of a community based on a commons that is offshore and dehumanised because it is purely technological. It also reduces shared communal action to networking. Yet, as Rémi Astruc indicates, human communities are not necessarily incompatible with ANT and are an absolute necessity, if not to take back control of industrial processes, at least to allow the development of approaches other than strictly competition-based ones, that are quantifiable by official statistical data and grounded in sharing: sharing an emotion before a work of art (Astruc 2015), sharing an experience lived collectively, or a shared experience of the mind in reading, thinking about a text or an idea. For what use are books, artworks and theories without an audience to share them with?

Faced with the awareness of a major environmental crisis, or even of an imminent apocalypse, Jewish mysticism, as demonstrated by Antonin Chambon, can contribute answers and hope grounded in the community, in as much as opening up to messianic times, considered as real or utopian, supposes a phase of total destruction. In the categories of Jewish mysticism and in the Tikkun Olam communities are not constituted based on a common, shared heritage (be it religious, cultural, economic, etc.), but from a sense of absence felt by all. Never mind if the messiah suggests a utopia not situated in time or a post-apocalyptic future, that he has always been there even if mankind was incapable of recognising him or is only revealed after the ultimate catastrophe, in any case it is his absence that guides people, unites them and incites them to improve the world... together. The communities born of this absence are thus not fixed groups linked by a shared particularity, but rather by a desire for shared action. They are process and sharing; a sharing that can authorise a more or less radical otherness (in Jewish mysticism) (Antonin Chambon), a temporality that can be very brief (in art) (Rémi Astruc), liberating energies for communal moments and collective actions generated by new interactions thanks to the social networks of web 2.0 (Radu Cinpoes). The articulation between local identity and the planetary scale as well as the major role of interconnected technology are also at the core of the study undertaken by Graham Roberts on the iconic representation conveyed by photography of Russian male fashion transmitted by Internet. By systematically going against the stereotype of the triumphant virility of the Russian male, the fashion designers Serguei Teplov, Cyrille Gassiline and Gosha Rubchinskiy who circulate their photographs via Internet, are a good incarnation of the increased demand by individuals for reflexivity highlighted by Radu Cinpoes and Margaret Archer. Faced with a strictly national definition of community, defined by the opposition between its own national stereotypes and those from elsewhere, which rejects otherness, these fashion designers propose the opposite: a form of connected community based on a transgender and transgressive otherness developed in the context of the global turn and the emergence of a gender question that goes beyond binary definitions.

These studies are of course only a step. They do not at all aim to exhaust the question of "the common" and communities based on their relation to globalisation, or offer a methodological approach that is an example to all. Rather, they seek to contribute to enlarging perspectives and identifying possible spaces for acting on the world in an inclusive manner, in considering not only humans on different scales but also the biosphere as a whole, and why not, the exploration of space and our relation to cosmic space.

References

Agamben Giorgio, *La comunità che viene*, Torino, Bollati Boringhieri, 2001.

Agamben Giorgio, *Qu'est-ce que le contemporain?*, Paris, Rivages, 2008.

Appadurai Arjun, *La condition de l'homme global*, Paris, Payot, 2013.

Astruc Rémi, *Nous? L'aspiration à la communauté des arts*, Versailles, RKI Press, 2015.

Balibar Étienne, Wallerstein Immanuel, *Race, nation, classe. Les identités ambiguës*, Paris, La Découverte, 1997.

Blanchot Maurice, *La communauté inavouable*, Paris, Minuit, 1983.

Butler Judith, *Rassemblement. Pluralité, performativité et politique*, Paris, Fayard, 2016.

Caillé Alain, Dufoix Stéphane (eds.), *Le tournant global des sciences sociales*, Paris, La Découverte, 2013.

Latour Bruno, *Face à Gaïa. Huit conférences sur le nouveau régime climatique*, Paris, La Découverte, 2015.

Mezzadra Sandro, *La condizione postcoloniale. Storia e politica nel presente globale*, Verona, Ombre corte, 2008.

Mignolo Walter (ed.), *La désobéissance épistémique. Rhétorique de la modernité, logique de la colonialité et grammaire de la colonialité*, Bruxelles, Peter Lang, 2015.

Nancy Jean-Luc, *Être singulier pluriel*, Paris, Galilée, 1996.

Nancy Jean-Luc (avec Bailly J.-C.), *La Comparution*, Paris, Christian Bourgois, 1991.

Robertson Roland, "Globalisation or glocalisation?", in *Journal of International Communication*, 1994, no.°1(1), p. 33–52.

Looking South. Forgotten constructions of the global

STÉPHANE DUFOIX

In the late 2000s, while I was completing my habilitation thesis about the uses of the word "diaspora" from the 3rd century before the Christian Era until present times (Dufoix 2017), I started working on the theories of globalization. My idea was to try and provide a historical sociology of how the very rapid spread of the concept of globalization from the early 1990s onwards had emerged from within the earlier philosophical and social debate about modernity (Dufoix 2013, 2018). From 2010 to roughly 2015, I organized two international conferences, one at the UNESCO in 2010 about the "global turn in the social sciences" (Caillé, Dufoix 2013), and a Cerisy symposium in 2015 about the "anti-utilitarian bases of the social sciences" (Caillé e.a. 2018); in the meantime, I also delivered a course entitled "Globalization and social sciences" at Sciences Po Paris from 2012 to 2015. This investigation gradually led me to distinguish between two different kinds of concepts of globalization, the first one insisting on the homogenizing process at play, and the second one emphasizing the heterogenizing process at play; the former seeing the global as something more encompassing – the "globality" – whereas the latter tried to move away from the uniformizing movement to rather concentrate on the importance of transnationalism and flows.

At that time, the opposition between these two big visions of globalization – although it also left some place for intermediate or compromising attempts – appeared to me as being the largest part of the new reflections about sociological theory. I only progressively realized that I was blind when I read – in 2012 – the Australian sociologist Raewyn Connell's "The Northern Theory of Globalization" (2007) and included it in the syllabus of my course to discuss it with my students. All of the sudden, and even more when I started looking at some other references from her bibliography, I realized that what I had previously seen as being the whole continent was but only one. I also realized – which I had never really been aware of during my sociological training – that sociology could be practiced differently in others parts of the world, and that global power relations at the world level had so much silenced some non-Western sociological voices in the last decades that they could not be heard in France. I started learning about new names and reading new authors (Aníbal Quijano, Ashis Nandy, Orlando Fals Borda, Syed Hussein Alatas, etc.), thus discovering completely unknown continents of thought. The more I worked on that almost completely hidden history, and the more it became clear to me that globalization actually did not belong to the history of thought as such but to the history of Northern thought being instrumentalized as the history of thought in general. What was true of globalization was also true of the social sciences in general[1].

A deep and effective genealogy of the history of social sciences – sociology (Bhambra 2014), anthropology (Ribeiro, Escobar 2006) and history (Goody 2006) – shows how much non-Western traditions of thought were silenced or suppressed by Western colonialism and/or scientific hegemony, thus leading to what the Indian political scientist Rajeev Bhargava (2013) has named the "epistemic injustice of colonialism". The existence of this structural inequality within the world production of social sciences was challenged quite early on – at least from the 1950s on – in Asia, Latin America, Africa or the Arab world. However, the global invisibility of these early reactions to Western hegemony in the social sciences remained the rule until the 1990s when the "indigenous" or "autonomous" perspective on the one hand (Akiwowo 1986; Alatas 2006), and the "decolonial" perspective on the other (Grosfoguel 2007) saw their opposition to Western epistemic hegemony grow more and more visible in the global academic field. Within the last ten years, this multiform and plural counter-hegemonic movement has but amplified itself, notably through various individual or collective voices in books or articles advocating the necessity to take into consideration the

---

[1]   The result of this eye-opening phase was the creation of a new course at Sciences Po entitled "Are Social Sciences Universal?", and that attempted at transmitting to students a wider panorama of the social sciences at the global level, not only nowadays but also in the previous decades.

diversity of traditions in the social sciences (in the case of sociology, see Burawoy, Chang, Hsieh 2010, Patel 2010).

Although this autobiographical detour may seem a bit odd here, it intends to shed some light on how Western academics usually tend to look at the global in only one way and therefore completely leave out of their reach a large number of older or contemporary visions that might enlarge our vision of today's social sciences if we accepted to open our eyes a bit broader.

Globalization as a Siamese twin concept

If the chronology of globalization as such has been the object of many debates, the most important thing lies in the fact that the word itself – and the concept – actually seemed not to appear and become widespread before the 1980s[2]. In contrast to what is usually considered, globalization was less born as a new field of study per se than as a new general perspective to rethink the relationship between spatiality and modernity. In this respect, the "global turn" of the social sciences also represents some form of a "spatial turn". To be sure, the extraordinarily rapid expansion of the uses of the words "global" and "globalization" from the early 1990s onwards is neither a sui generis invention nor the simple reflection in the academic world of some visible transformations of the world at one specific moment in time as though. It has instead taken shape within a whole set of interrogations – about the future of capitalism, about human condition, about risks at the world level, about identities, about the practice of disciplines, etc. If all of those interrogations could be distinct from one another, they gradually became more and more entangled in the larger debate about the nature and the future of modernity that became more and more important in the human and social sciences throughout the 1980s.

Within the field of sociology, this fundamental debate about changes in and of the world – and about its potential consequences for the discipline – was at the heart of the organization of the International Sociological Association (ISA) World Congress that took place in Madrid in 1990

---

[2] Some earlier mentions could be found. For "globalization", see Capdepuy (2011) and Dufoix (2013). For the interesting case of "mondialisation" in late 1940s France, see Dufoix and Foucher-Dufoix (2016).

around the topic "Globalization, Knowledge and Society". All the participants get a copy of a small book bearing the same title and composed with a selection of some articles published in the *International Sociology* journal between 1986 et 1990 (Albrow, King 1990). In her preface to that book, the President of the ISA, Margaret Archer, insists on the fact that "globalization is the present process of becoming global: globality itself lies in the future, but the very near future" (Archer 1990: 1). This change is not understood as something trivial but as an essential transformation that will affect the practice of sociology: "For just as we cannot remain the national practitioners that we once were, neither can we hang on to the old tools of the trade, continuing to think and to theorise as we once did" (*ibid.*).

Another question that became important is that of the link that should exist between the social transformations at the planetary level – the impression of the advent of "new world" – and classical sociological theory. Here again, the answer is not one. As I recently showed it elsewhere (Dufoix 2018), "globalization" was born in the late 1980s and very early 1990s as a twin concept, two completely distinct and almost contradictory versions of globalization being brandished: globalization as a continuity within the whole process of world-making and within the conceptual history of the social sciences, and globalization as a rupture within those same processes. Just like Charles Cooley could write more than one century ago that "self and society are twin-born" (Cooley 1909: 5), the social science of globalization was born in the shape of Siamese Janus-faced twins who would share part of a single body while looking into different directions. The agreement on the word tends to hide a whole set of contradictions in the interpretation of the phenomenon, not only about the prevalence of homogenization or heterogenization trends, but also about the form of modernity involved or, which is our main interest here, the future of sociological tradition.

According to a first group comprising sociologists like Anthony Giddens (1990) or Roland Robertson (1992) – the latter being one of the very first social scientists using the concept of globalization from the early 1980s – the tools and concepts of classical sociology can perfectly be re-elaborated, re-thought and adapted to the study of globalization, all the more so because the sociology developed by the founders was not as parochial as it was later denounced and actually possessed a real global horizon (Pendenza 2014). The idea of classical sociology having to be reconsidered so that its genuine global ambition might be visible gradually appears as some way to both ensure the preservation of the sociological tradition and its possible move towards a sociology of the global without having to choose between both and therefore provoke a divide between sociologists. This does imply going back to the classics. As Bryan Turner wrote in the late 1980s, "sociology itself has to break out of its nationalistic and parochial concerns with particular nation-states from a society-centered perspective" (Turner 1989: 636). In this respect, the link between the 19th century and the late 20th century is elaborated through the prism of globalism and humanity:

> Perhaps the crisis which drove intellectuals at the end of the nineteenth century into sociology, socialism and internationalism might, however, also find an echo in our epoch. Durkheim's reflections on Saint-Simon's vision of the necessity for European integration, an end to English aggression against the European continent and a new science of humanity might be a valuable point of departure for contemporary social sciences to begin to engage (once again) with the tensions between our local concerns with national issues and our vocation, albeit underdeveloped and ill-defined, for a global sociology of humanity (Turner 1990: 356).

According to Turner (1990), the "two faces of sociology" – that is, national and global – have to be understood as the two faces of the same coin and not as opposite projects as some other sociologists intend to understand it.

The second conception is best exemplified in the works of such authors as Stuart Hall, Arjun Appadurai and Ulrich Beck, both in their analysis of the contemporary situation and of the epistemological challenges faced by social scientists in order to account of the changes of and in the world. In this respect, words like "cosmopolitanism", "transnationalism" or "diasporas" find a new and crucial place in the conceptual architecture of a new social science that needs to be properly distinguished from the outdated, classical and national-oriented social science.

If the British sociologist Stuart Hall has become world-famous for his works on culture and identity, his study of these two themes in the context of globalization are lesser known (Hall 1992). His vision of culture, ethnicity, diaspora and identity cannot be dissociated with his perception of "new times" (Hall 1989a) bringing about new identities and ethnicities. In two talks delivered in the Spring 1989 (1991a, 1991b), he insisted on how globalization meant important transformations of the relationship between the local and the global, and thus important modifications of the meanings of identity and ethnicity, since those two could not be understood any more within the old stable and fixed traditional definition, and had to be analyzed across boundaries and across frontiers (Hall 1991a: 38).

In this logic, the old academic conception of identity had to be replaced by a new one that might closely fit the transformations of identities themselves, less homogeneous and more hybrid. He considered that "the great collective social identities which we thought of as large-scale, all-encompassing, homogenous, as unified collective identities", such as class, race, nation, gender, and the West, have indeed not disappeared, but "none of them is, any longer, in either the social, historical or epistemological place where they were in our conceptualizations of the world in the recent past. They cannot any longer be thought in the same homogenous form" (Hall 1991b: 44–45). For Hall, globalization is thus characterized by two ongoing processes, one that heads towards more homogenization, and another one that heads in the other direction towards the production of more and more differences.

At the same time, in the late 1980s, alone or with his anthropologist wife Carol Breckenridge, the Indian-American Arjun Appadurai worked in the same direction as Stuart Hall. In 1988, Breckenridge and he launched the journal *Public Culture*. Reading some of the editorials they wrote for the first issues is quite telling about their vision of what globalization means. If these texts are not among the most famous by either authors, they do give us an inestimable access to the making of a new way of thinking about the world, a new way that emphasizes a new lexicon as well, or that at least reconfigures an older lexicon, especially about "diaspora" or "modernity" (see Dufoix 2017). The very first lines of their editorial in the first issue of *Public Culture* set the tone:

> Our principal goal in starting this journal is to create an intellectual forum for interaction among those concerned with global cultural flows. Such flows, by their nature, are reflected in the emergent public cultures of many nation-states. Furthermore, these public cultures constitute the centers of new forms of cosmopolitanism in many linguistic and cultural ecumenes (Appadurai, Breckenridge 1988a: 1).

As the "the world of the late twentieth century is increasingly a cosmopolitan world" (Appadurai, Breckenridge 1988b: 5), they promoted a new conceptual vocabulary. This reframing of concepts was for instance, just like Stuart Hall did at the same time (Hall 1989b), directed at the

concept of diaspora in a later editorial: "Indeed, to speak of diasporas –
if by diasporas we mean phenomena involving stable points of origin,
clear and final destinations and coherent group identities – seems already
part of a sociology for the world we have lost" (Appadurai, Breckenridge
1989: I). In his own personal research, Arjun Appadurai came to the
same conclusions, especially in a 1990 article in which he assumed that
"the central problem of today's global interactions is the tension between
cultural homogenization and cultural heterogenization" (Appadurai
1990: 295). The vocabulary-reconfiguring enterprise notably took the
shape of the famous five "-scapes" (ethnoscapes, mediascapes, financ-
escapes, ideoscapes and technoscapes) that are supposed to replace the
older concepts of identity, ethnicity, territory etc. (see Appadurai 1996).

One of the best illustrations of this intention to replace an old vision
of the social science by a new one in order to better fit to the world
emerging is the German sociologist Ulrich Beck's position in defense
of what he called "methodological cosmopolitanism", which he considered as being the new paradigm for social science (see Beck 2000,
2006, 2011). Taking up on the Portuguese sociologist Herminio Martins' (1974) notion of "methodological nationalism", he made it the
main characteristic of modern and classical sociology with its emphasis
on the nation-state, on territory and on sovereignty. If this perspective
might have been relevant for the study of modern national societies, it
could not be accurate to analyze the new world of global flows and risks.
Conversely, the new methodological cosmopolitanism should pay much
more attention to spatiality, alterity, inequalities and differences.

At first sight, it may appear that the latter conceptions were more
global and thus provided a better encompassing of the diversity of the
world. However, it was rapidly criticized for its Western or Northern
(Connell 2007) flavor. In 2011, the Indian sociologist Sujata Patel came
to terms with Ulrich Beck's methodological cosmopolitanism on the
ground that this notion, despite its ambition of moving towards a less
"modern" and more "fluid" understanding of the world, took it for
granted that the whole was moving from a national to a cosmopolitan
lens. Defending the idea that "unfortunately the terms 'cosmopolitan'/
'cosmopolitanism' and 'global' have had a long history within European
modernities and remain overburdened with these histories and thus
their meanings" (Patel 2011: 13), she actually emphasized the fact that
the necessity for Southern sociologists to defend their particularity in
relation to Western epistemic domination resulted in the valorization

of national or localized sociologies that nevertheless did not renounce a connection with scientific universalism.

A specific local-global nexus in Southern sociology. Relevance and universalism

The challenge to universalism and dependency and the calls for relevance did not start in the recent period (Alatas 1995), and many examples can be found of earlier stands for the recovery of independence or autonomy in the realm of thought in general, and social science in particular. In 1899, the Argentinian social scientist Juan Agustín García, who would teach social sciences at the University of Buenos Aires, attempted to map out the broad lines thereof "from an exclusively national point of view [...] in order to show the students that forming Argentinian social sciences is feasible and that our economic, social and political phenomena are just as interesting as those of the Europeans", adding to this that the persistence in using the most classical approaches to study the new countries is a "serious mistake" because "the social fact out there are obviously original" (García 1907: 5–6, my translation). In the same vein, in another part of the work, the Indian philosopher Krishna Chandra Bhattacharya (1977) stated in 1931 that self-determination – using the Hindi word *swaraj* that was at the time the rallying word for Indian independence – was fundamental in the realm of ideas, while, at about the same time in China, the sociologist Sun Benwen (Dirlik 2012: 17) and the anthropologist Wu Wenzao (Chen 2018: 23–24) were also trying to "sinicize" their disciplines. But these attempts were mostly scattered and did not necessarily imply a more general reconceptualization of what social sciences were and of what its foundational principles should be.

It does not necessarily mean that these engagements for a more "relevant", "national", "original" or "specific" social science or sociology were necessarily opposing sociologist from the North to sociologists of the South. The Brazilian case in the 1950s is quite emblematic in this respect, since the opposition between two opposite visions of sociology, a "universal" one on the one hand, and a "national" one on the other, did not come from a Western and a non-Western sociologist, but rather from two Brazilian sociologists, thus demonstrating the fractal dimension of a universal scientific definition of social science that is not confined to the Western world. The debate between the Western-oriented sociologist Florestan Fernandes and the Brazilian-oriented sociologist Alberto Guerreiro Ramos cannot even be summarized as being a mere opposition between universalism and particularism. During the second Latin-American Congress of sociology that was held in Rio in 1953, Guerreiro Ramos listed seven propositions for sociology, among which the necessity not to simply transplant sociological methods adopted in developed countries, as well as the role of teaching sociology in students' cultural emancipation (Ramos 1957: 77–78). If those propositions were refused by the participants to the Congress (Bariani 2006: 152, Lynch 2015: 155–156), Guerreiro Ramos' engagement against foreign categories and concepts and for a sociological universalism initiated a disputed debate – although mostly indirect – between him and Florestan Fernandes, the latter being the French sociologist Roger Bastide's successor at the University of São Paulo. In 1958, both defended their own perspective on sociological science using such expressions as "national sociology" or "universal" but the meaning they associated to it was largely different. For Fernandes, there was indeed the necessity of a Brazilian – that is, national – sociology but it should not be "nationalist" lest it should move away from the "pattern of scientific work" that makes sociology a positivist science characterized by the universality of its reasoning and of its techniques (Fernandes 1958: 57 sq.).

In his book *A Redução sociològica. The Sociological Reduction* (1996), published in 1958 too, Guerreiro Ramos stated what he called the "laws of sociological reduction". There were four of them: engagement; subsidiary character of foreign scientific production; universality of scientific general statements; and the law of the phases. It is important to briefly summarize the first three of them.

The law of engagement offers a distinction between engagement as such and compromise. According to Ramos, engaging into the social reality of one's country is not a betrayal of the scientific ideal: conversely, it can be understood as some way to reach a "forthcoming" universal, a universal that would not be disconnected from what is happening in other countries of the world, for every human being is not only a "being in the world" but also a historically situated: "Insofar as it is systematic, the engagement we're talking about situates the scholar in the universal perspective of the human community" (Ramos 1996: 106, my translation)[3].

---

[3] On the importance of the notion of "universal human community" in the works of Alberto Guerreiro Ramos, see Flores (2015).

The law about the subsidiary character of every foreign scientific production postulated, on the basis of Husserl's phenomenology, that every
"cultural object" always presents itself under different shapes depending
on the different cultures. These cultural objects "are not universal para-
digms and therefore they cannot be transferred from one [...] perspective
to the other" (*ibid.*: 114, my translation) unless they become reduced so
as to be adaptable to another cultural perspective. The consequence for
sociology is crucial since it implies for Guerreiro Ramos that sociological
systems have always first and foremost been elaborated *for* one society
in particular and not universally: "This *for* is the very meaning of the
sociological product in question. First of all, Spencer's system is meaningful for the English. Comte's system for the French. Weber's for the
Germans. And Lester Ward's for North-Americans" (Ramos 1996: 115,
my translation).

The objective of the law about the universality of general statements
is to precise the link that exists between general scientific reasoning and
the specific practice of sociologists in the countries where they live, thus
recalling the essential relationship existing between a sociologist and his
belonging to a national society. As Guerreiro Ramos bluntly puts it, "the
negation of the existence of national sociologies is almost always practiced in the name of a false universalism" (*ibid.*: 125). He thus establishes a more complex relationship between two terms that are usually
opposed: classical universalism can be relativized and brought back to the
social and local conditions of its production, while nationalism, under
certain circumstances, can keep in touch with the universal. According
to him, the sociologist is a "being in situation", which ineluctably links
his capacity to reason and the content of his reasoning to the situation
of the country – of the society – in which he lives. Only the recognition
of this "colonial" – or "dependent" as it would later be called – situation
of Brazil would allow to find the appropriate means not to be "mentally
colonized" anymore and to move from the status of "passive consumer of
ideas" to that of "producer of new ideas" (*ibid.*: 126).

This articulation between the local and the global or, to be more
precise here, between the particular and the universal in the field of
human and social sciences, has to be understood properly. On the whole,
it reflects less an attempt at absolutely de-universalizing the world of
science that at transforming the rules of the epistemic game. Despite
their potential connection to the broader world of international organi-
zations – such as the International Sociological Association since the late

1940s –, the instances cited above are national and mostly nationally-oriented. There seems to be no real connection of those various epistemic resistances and/or alternatives until the early 1970s when a number of different political and geopolitical factors coalesced and created the conditions of possibility for a gradual and growing connectivity between scholars from the so-called "developing world". The "rise of the Third World" was epitomized by the organization of the Bandoeng Conference in 1955 and the creation in 1964 of the United Nations Conference on Trade and Development (UNCTAD) led by the Argentinian economist Raúl Prebisch – who was also heading the United Nations Economic Commission for Latin America (in Spanish CEPAL) – and working for the establishment of new rules of the economic game at the international level. Within the UNCTAD, the Group of 77, that first gathered the Afro-Asian countries before extending to Latin American countries, was responsible for the drafting of the UN Resolution about the New international economic order that would be voted in 1974. In the latter, the p) point of the 4th section considered as a fundamental principle the fact of "giving to the developing countries access to the achievements of modern science and technology, and promoting the transfer of technology and the creation of indigenous technology for the benefit of the developing countries in forms and in accordance with procedures which are suited to their economies".

This insistence on "indigenous technology", that is quite often related to other terms or phrases like "endogenous", "indigeneity", "endogeneity", "indigenous" or "endogenous development" is fundamental for that period for it signals the growing emergence of a lexicon that both aims at challenging the homogenizing discourses about economic, political, social and technological modernization and at providing an alternative framework that would take into consideration the various specificities of societies and cultural formations. This vocabulary of "indigenization" has quite often been considered as entailing a real risk of fragmenting the various disciplines (psychology, anthropology, political science or sociology) and thus dangerously threatening the universal meaning of science The following sections would like to show that some of the networks created by Third World scholars during the 1970s in order to defend the idea of endogeneity were not national or local associations defending it for one place in particular as though "indigenous" was tantamount of "endemic". All the contrary, whether they had been the result of academics that had been eager to meet up, exchange and act together, or the product of a program coming from an international institution, it was always a transnational enterprise.

The example of the Third World Forum is quite interesting in this respect. Founded in Karachi in 1975 with Samir Amin at its head after a first meeting in Santiago de Chile in 1973, it gathered a number of Third World social scientists coming from various continents. Even though the Santiago Declaration asks for "the search of more relevant development strategies", not only does it present itself as a "creative interaction between indigenous thinking and external experience"[4], but the various scholars that were present insisted on their will to become an Intellectual Forum of the Third World, which they became two years later[5]. Among the participants – mostly economists at the times – there were not only Latin-Americans like the Chilean economist Osvaldo Sunkel or the Uruguayan current director of the CEPAL Enrique Iglesias but also academics from the Arab World like the Egyptian Samir Amin, the Nigerian economist H.M.A Onitiri, the Pakistani Mahbub Ul Haq, the Indian economist Jagdish Bhagwati and his wife, the Indian economist Padma Desai (Devés 2006).

Another important body in this respect was the International Social Science Council (ISSC)[6], that was instrumental in creating connections, helping associations, organizing meetings etc. Though still an underestimated and understudied body as far as the evolution of international social science is concerned, it was crucial in putting people together. The 1975–1979 period, under the chairmanship of the Norwegian political scientist Stein Rokkan – who had been very active in the ISA as a General Secretary and later as a member of the Executive Committee – is of great importance since Rokkan launched a number of programs for social scientists in the developing countries that had implications at the

---

[4]   "Santiago Declaration of Third World Social Scientists", reproduced in Todaro (1977: 411).

[5]   The Karachi communique announcing the creation and the program of the Third World Forum can be found in Erb and Kallab (1975: 178–182).

[6]   The ISSC was founded in 1952 under the aegis of the UNESCO as a federation of five and then six international social science associations – the International Association of Legal Science, the International Economic Association (IEA), the International Political Science Association (IPSA), the International Sociological Association (ISA) and the International Union of Scientific Psychology, to which was added the International Union of Anthropological and Ethnological Sciences in 1953. On the ISSC, see Rokkan (1979) and Platt (2002).

global level, and especially at the Third World level. The first one was the Equalization Fund that would allow Third World scholars to ask for the funding of their travels to international conferences or meetings. The second one was the Group of Twenty on Man's Social Condition[7] that included people like the Egyptian economist Samir Amin, the Mexican anthropologist Pablo Gonzalez Casanova, the Philippine demographer Mercedes Concepcion, the Brazilian lawyer Helio Jaguaribe, the Indian political scientist Rajni Kothari, the Indian sociologist M.N. Srinivas, the Mexican anthropologist Rodolfo Stavenhagen and the economist Puey Ungphakorn from Thailand[8]. The third, and certainly most relevant one for our study is the creation of the World Social Science Development Committee that was thus presented in the summary report of its first meeting in Rio de Janeiro in November-December 1975:

> The Committee sees its functions as comprising, for the countries of Africa, Asian, and Latin America:
>
> (1) the development of the social sciences and a body of social scientists in a manner which makes them more relevant or relevant to their societies;
> (2) the identification of problems confronting social scientists and societies in the countries;
> (3) the initiation of action to meet some of the most urgent problems confronting the social scientists and society;
> (4) the contribution to a truly international system of social sciences[9].

Once again, it is important to insist on the fact that the committee is – not surprisingly – composed of mostly Third World scholars. Among the names are to be found the Malaysian political scientist K.J. Ratnam (who was part of the Kyoto symposium in 1978), Enrique Oteiza (who was part of the Third World Forum from the very beginning and wrote the report on cooperation in Latin America for the UNESCO at the Paris conference in 1976), the Brazilian sociologist Fernando Henrique Cardoso, The Indian sociologist and President of the Indian council of

---

[7] For the Group of 20 project, see ISSC Archives, ISSC/2/6.12: ISSC projects, 1975–1983. The project apparently aborted.

[8] "Group of Twenty on Man's Social Condition", list of members dated October 1975, ISSC Archives, ISSC/2/6.12, 3 p.

[9] First meeting of the World Social Science Development, Rio de Janeiro, 29 November-4 December 1975, Summary Report, ISSC archives, ISSC/2/6.13: ISSC projects, 1975–1979, p. 1–2.

social science research M.S. Gore, the Philippine psychologist Estefania Aldaba-Lim, the Egyptian sociologist Leila al-Hamsasy or the Congolese specialist of pedagogy Jean-Kanga Kalemba-Vita.

At about the same time, the relationship between development and endogeneity found a new path in 1976 with the opening in Tokyo of the United Nations University (UNU), a project that had been discussed within the UNESCO from the late 1960s and formally established in 1973. In 1975, a program entitled Human and Social Development (HSDP) was developed within the UNU with the Japanese political scientist Kinhide Mushakoji at its head (Mushakoji 1988: 171–179), that gave birth in 1977 to a specific project – named Socio-Cultural Development Alternatives in a Changing World (SCA) – under the scientific supervision of the Egyptian economist and sociologist Anouar Abdel-Malek[10]. This project unfolded into two sub-projects, the first one being Endogenous Intellectual Creativity, and the second one Transformations of the World. The SCA project linked together many researchers from diverse parts of the world (Asia, Latin America, the Arab world, Eastern and Central Europe) between 1978 and 1982 in several conferences held in Kyoto, Belgrade, Mexico or Kuwait City. To give but one example, the first regional conference on "endogenous intellectual creativity", that was held in Kyoto (13–17 November 1978), gathered 67 participants coming from nearly 20 countries: Singapore, Indonesia, India, Japan, China, Philippines, France, Malaysia, the USA, Vietnam, Thailand, Afghanistan, Kuwait, Brazil, Mexico, Canada, Fiji, Great-Britain and Yugoslavia (Abdel-Malek, Pandeya 1980).

Among many topics pertaining to relevance or "endogenous creativity" in general, the symposia constituted a collective – mostly but non-only Southern – opportunity to talk about the transformations of the world and about "globalization", a term that was already widely used at the time to describe the growing influence of capitalism all over the world in some of these SCA conferences (see in particular Gonzalez, del Campo Urbano, Mesa 1984). In contradiction to what I had been writing so far about the first consolidated uses of *globalization* and *global* (Dufoix 2013, 2018), it seems that these late 1970s transnational debates were already a forum for discussing the future of a world confronted to

---

[10]   On the important figure of Anouar Abdel-Malek, who lived in France since the late 1950s, and his connection with the UNESCO, see Brisson (2008).

important globalizing processes of various kinds. If some contributions to the symposium clearly focus on "national" intellectual traditions, the search for endogenous academic development is also counterbalanced by a pragmatic emphasis on the necessity not to confound endogeneity and nativism in the social sciences. Thus, Kawano Kenji, the then Director of the Institute for Research in Institute for Humanities at Kyoto University, insists on the importance of mutual relations between researchers and conceptions of social science:

> But we have to realize that the idea that every nation has a unique and genuine culture originating from within is only a misconception deriving from the ideology of traditionalism. No culture can develop solely by its own force without influencing and being influenced by others. [...] We should not mistake "endogeneity" with "genuineness" or "closeness". "Endogeneity" should be compatible with "globalness" (Kawano 1980: 12).

In his contribution about "alternative development", the Argentine sociologist Jorge Graciarena, one of the early experts within the HSDP, evokes the transformations of the world towards a "planetary society": "However, this 'globalization' of the world does not hide in any way its internal diversity and even less the inequalities that prevail in it" (Graciarena 1984: 11). The link between globality and cultural diversity is absolutely crucial in this respect. Acknowledging this diversity – what Celso Furtado (1984a: 122) calls the "fabulous potential of human inventiveness" – and promoting endogenous cultural development is a way to reach a different universalism than the one proclaimed by the West: "This project [HSDP] is thus exactly the opposite of the colonial enterprises that destroyed civilizations. From the most different locations in the world, it lays out the possibility and the necessity to create a more humane and really universal civilization" (González Casanova 1984b: XI).

The short developments above do not only constitute an invitation to think differently about the global and globalization and to revise our beliefs about their recent conceptual inception in the early 1990s. It is first and foremost an invitation to see how our concepts are rhetorical weapons in a larger environment, in which the defense of an alternative definition of, say, universalism is both an epistemological and political standpoint, just as is the promotion of endogeneity, indigeneity or particularism. In this respect, a more relevant vision of the epistemic world at the global level nowadays should pay more attention to what has been going on in the so-called developing world during the last decades – and maybe even earlier – instead of often considering it as a mere imitation of Western social sciences or as a mere political gesture that should not have a place of its own within the academic global world. More careful insights into the non-Western or non-Northern evolution of what had been called "sociology" for a long time, and not only since the postwar period (see Dufoix, Macé 2019), would give us an access to a whole different world of globalness and specificity where both terms are not standing in opposition to one another but forming a more complex – and yet more invisible too – nexus that could be very helpful in the forthcoming and necessary process of decolonizing social sciences.

References

Abdel-Malek Anouar, Amar Nath Pandeya (eds.), *Intellectual Creativity in Endogenous Culture*, Tokyo, The United Nations University, 1980.

Akiwowo Akinsola, "Contribution to the Sociology of Knowledge from an African Oral Poetry", in *International Sociology*, no.°1(4), 1986, p. 343–358.

Alatas Syed Farid, "The Theme of 'Relevance' in Third World Human Sciences", in *Singapore Journal of Tropical Geography*, no.°16(2), 1995, p. 123–140.

Alatas Syed Hussein, "The Autonomous, the Universal and the Future of Sociology", in *Current Sociology*, no.°54(1), 2006, p. 7–23.

Albrow Martin, Elizabeth King (eds.), *Globalization, Knowledge and Society: Readings from International Sociology*, London, Sage, 1990.

Appadurai Arjun, "Editors' Comments", in *Public Culture*, no. 1(1), 1988a, p. 1–4.

Appadurai Arjun, "Why Public Culture?", in *Public Culture*, no. 1(1), 1988b, p. 5–9.

Appadurai Arjun, "Disjuncture and Difference in the Global Cultural Economy", in *Theory, Culture and Society*, no. 7(2), 1990, p. 295–310.

Appadurai Arjun, *Modernity at Large: Cultural Dimensions of Globalization*, Minneapolis, University of Minnesota Press, 1996.

Appadurai Arjun, Carol Breckenridge, "Editors' Comments: On Moving Targets", in *Public Culture*, no. 2(1), p. I–IV.

Archer Margaret, "Foreword", in Albrow Martin, Elizabeth King (eds.), *Globalization, Knowledge and Society*, London, Sage, 1990, p. 1–2.

Bariani Edison, "Padrão e salvação. o debate Florestan Fernandes x Guerreiro Ramos", in *Cronos*, no. 7(1), 2006, p. 151–160.

Beck Ulrich, "The Cosmopolitan Perspective: Sociology of the Second Age of Modernity", in *British Journal of Sociology*, no. 51(1), 2000, p. 79–105.

Beck Ulrich, *The Cosmopolitan Vision*, Cambridge, Polity Press (1st German edition 2004), 2006.

Beck Ulrich, "Cosmopolitan Sociology: Outline of a Paradigm Shift", in Nowicka Magdalena, Maria Rovisco (eds.), in *The Ashgate Research Companion to Cosmopolitanism*, Burlington, Ashgate, 2011, p. 17–32.

Bhambra Gurminder, *Connected Sociologies*, London, Bloomsbury, 2014.

Bhargava Rajeev, "Pour en finir avec l'injustice épistémique du colonialisme", in *Socio*, no. 1, 2013, p. 41–75.

Bhattacharya Krishna Chandra, "Swaraj in Ideas" [1931], in Ghose Sisinkumar (ed.), *Four Indian Critical Essays: K. C. Bhattacharya, B.N. Seal, Rabindranath Tagore, Sri Aurobindo*, Calcutta, Jijnasa, 1977, p. 13–22.

Brisson Thomas, *Les Intellectuels arabes et la France*, Paris, La Dispute, 2008.

Burawoy Michael, Mau-kuei Chang, Michelle Fei-yu Hsieh (eds.), *Facing an Unequal World: Challenges for A Global Sociology*, 3 vol., Taipei, Academia Sinica, 2010.

Caillé Alain, Philippe Chanial, Stéphane Dufoix, Frédéric Vandenberghe (eds.), *Des sciences sociales à la science sociale*, Paris, Le Bord de l'eau, 2018.

Caillé Alain, Stéphane Dufoix (eds.), *Le Tournant global des sciences sociales*, Paris, La Découverte, 2013.

Capdepuy Vincent, "Au prisme des mots. La mondialisation et l'argument philologique", in *Cybergeo: European Journal of Geography*, no. 576, 2011, https://journals.openedition.org/cybergeo/24903.

Chen Hon-Fai, *Chinese Sociology. State-Building and the Institutionalization of Globally Circulated Knowledge*, London, Palgrave Macmillan, 2018.

Connell Raewyn, "The Northern Theory of Globalization", in *Sociological Theory*, no. 25(4), 2007, p. 368–385.

Cooley Charles, *Social Organization. A Study of the Larger Mind*, New York, Charles Scribner's Sons, 1909.

Devés Eduardo, "Los cientistas económico sociales chilenos en los largos 60 y su inserción en las redes internacionales: la reunión del foro tercer mundo en Santiago en abril de 1973", in *Universum. Revista de Humanidades y Ciencias Sociales*, no. 1(21), 2006, p. 1–34.

Dirlik Arif, "*Zhongguohua*: Worlding China. The Case of Sociology and Anthropology in 20th-century China", in *Sociology and Anthropology in Twentieth-Century China: Between Universalism and Indigenism*, Dirlik Arif, Li Guannan and Hsiao-Pei Yen (eds.), Hong Kong, The Chinese University Press, 2012, p. 1–39.

Dufoix Stéphane, "Les naissances académiques du global", in Caillé Alain, Stéphane Dufoix, *Le Tournant global des sciences sociales*, Paris, La Découverte, 2013, p. 27–43.

Dufoix Stéphane, *The Dispersion. A History of the Word Diaspora*, Leiden, Brill (1st French edition 2012), 2017.

Dufoix Stéphane, "Premiers éléments pour une sociologie historique des théories de la globalisation", in Caillé Alain, Philippe Chanial, Stéphane Dufoix, Frédéric Vandenberghe (eds.), *Des sciences sociales à la science sociale*, Paris, Le Bord de l'eau, 2018, p. 249–263.

Dufoix Stéphane, Éric Macé, "Les enjeux d'une sociologie mondiale non-hégémonique", in *Zilsel*, no. 5, 2019, p. 89–121.

Dufoix Stéphane, Valérie Foucher-Dufoix, "D'une mondialisation oubliée. Les postérités ambiguës de Cahors-Mundi", in *Ethnologie française*, no. 163, 2016, p. 537–553.

Erb Guy F., Valeriana Kallab (eds.), *Beyond Dependency: The Developing World Speaks Out*, Washington, Overseas Development Council, 1975.

Fernandes Florestan, *O padrão de trabalho científico dos sociológos brasileiros*, Rio de Janeiro, Edicões da Revista brasileira de estudos politicos, 1958.

Flores Elio Chaves, "O conceito de "comunidade humana universal" na obra de Guerreiro Ramos", in *Cadernos EBAPE.FR*, no. 13, 2015, p. 573–592.

Furtado Celso, "Creatividad cultural y desarrollo dependiente", in Pablo González Casanova (ed.), *Cultura y creación intelectual en América Latina*, México, Siglo Veintiuno Editores, 1984, p. 122–129.

García Juan Agustín, *Introducción al estudio de las ciencias sociales argentinas*, Buenos Aires, Ángel Estrada y Cía (1st edition 1899), 1907.

Giddens Anthony, *The Consequences of Modernity*, Cambridge, Polity Press, 1990.

González Casanova Pablo (ed.), *Cultura y creación intelectual en América Latina*, México, Siglo Veintiuno Editores, 1984a.

González Casanova Pablo, "Palabras introductorias", in González Casanova Pablo (ed.), *Cultura y creación intelectual en América Latina*, México, Siglo Veintiuno Editores, 1984b, p. IX–XI.

Gonzalez Mike, Salustiano del Campo Urbano, Roberto Mesa (eds.), *Economy and Society in the Transformation of the World*, London, Macmillan (in association with the United Nations University), 1984.

Goody Jack, *The Theft of History*, Cambridge, Cambridge University Press, 2006.

Graciarena Jorge, "Creación intellectual, estilos alternativos de desarrollo y futuro de la civilización industrial", in González Casanova Pablo (ed.), *Cultura y creación intelectual en América Latina*, México, Siglo Veintiuno Editores, 1984, p. 1–24.

Grosfoguel Ramón, "The Epistemic Decolonial Turn", in *Cultural Studies*, no. 21(2–3), 2007, p. 211–223.

Hall Stuart, "The Meaning of New Times", in Hall Stuart, J. Martin (eds.), *New Times*, London, Lawrence & Wishart, 1989a, p. 116–133.

Hall Stuart, "Cultural Identity and Diaspora", in *Framework*, no. 36, 1989b, p. 68–81.

Hall Stuart, "The Local and the Global: Globalization and Ethnicity", in King Anthony (ed.), *Culture, Globalization and the World-System. Contemporary Conditions for the Representation of Identity*, Binghamton, State University of New York, 1991a, p. 19–39.

Hall Stuart, "Old and New Identities, Old and New Ethnicities", in *Culture, Globalization and the World-System. Contemporary Conditions for the Representation of Identity*, King Anthony (ed.), Binghamton, State University of New York, 1991b, p. 14–68.

Hall Stuart, "The Question of Cultural Identity", in *Modernity and Its Futures*, Hall Stuart, David Held, Anthony McGrew (eds.), Cambridge, Polity Press/The Open University, 1992, p. 273–316.

Kawano Kenji, "Endogeneity and Globalness of Culture", in Abdel-Malek Anouar, Amar Nath Pandeya (eds.), *Intellectual Creativity in Endogenous Culture*, Tokyo, The United Nations University, 1980, p. 10–13.

Lynch Christian Edward Cyril, "Teoria pós-colonial e pensamento brasileiro na obra de Guerreiro Ramos: o pensamento sociológico (1953–1955)", in *Caderno CRH*, no. 28(73), 2015, p. 27–45.

Martins Herminio, "Time and Theory in Sociology", in Rex John (ed.), *Approaches to Sociology*, London, Routledge and Kegan, 1974, p. 246–294.

Mushakoji Kinhide, *Global Issues and Inter-Paradigmatic Dialogues. Essays on Multipolar Politics*, Torino, Albert Meynier Editore, 1988.

Patel Sujata (ed.), *The ISA Handbook of Diverse Sociological Traditions*, London, Sage, 2010.

Patel Sujata, "An International Sociology with Diverse Epistemes", in *Global Dialogue*, no. 1(4), 2011, p. 12–13.

Pendenza Massimo (ed.), *Classical Sociology beyond Methodological Nationalism*, Leiden, Brill, 2014.

Platt Jennifer, *Fifty Years of the International Social Science Council*, Paris, ISSC, 2002.

Ramos Alberto Guerreiro, *Introdução crítica à sociologia brasileira*, Rio de Janeiro, Andes, 1957.

Ramos Alberto Guerreiro, *A Redução sociológica* [1958], Rio de Janeiro, Editora UFRJ, 1996.

Ratnam K.J., "Endogenous Intellectual Creativity in the Social Sciences", in Abdel-Malek Anouar, Amar Nath Pandeya (eds.), *Intellectual Creativity in Endogenous Culture*, Tokyo, The United Nations University, 1980, p. 116–140.

Ribeiro Gustavo Lins, Arturo Escobar (eds.), *World Anthropologies. Disciplinary Transformations within Systems of Power*, Oxford, Berg, 2006.

Robertson Roland, *Globalization: Social Theory and Global Culture*, London, Sage, 1992.

Rokkan Stein (ed.), *A Quarter Century of International Social Science*, New Delhi, Concept Publishing Co, 1979.

Todaro Michael P., *Economic Development in the Third World*, London, Longman, 1977.

Turner Bryan S., "From Orientalism to Global Sociology", in *Sociology*, no. 23(4), 1989, p. 629–638.

Turner Bryan S., "The Two Faces of Sociology: Global or National?", in *Theory, Culture & Society*, no. 7(2–3), 1990, p. 343–358.

Meta-reflexivity and social mobilisation in action: Greta Thunberg and the *School Strike for Climate* movement

Radu Cinpoes

Introduction

This chapter offers a contribution to the central reflections advanced in this volume with regard to how new communities emerge and operate in the current global age. It aims to investigate different kinds of social interaction that take place at transnational level. Specifically, the chapter employs a framework that rests on critical realism and more precisely on the morphogenetic approach (Morphogenesis/Morphostasis or MM) developed by Margaret Archer (Archer 1988, 1995, 2000) as a meta-theory, or otherwise put as an explanatory programme that enables us to theorise about social change. It employs the concept of reflexivity and the notion of a "reflexive imperative" (Archer 2007, 2012) according to which societal transformations associated with late modernity have generated an increased demand for reflexivity from individuals, and by contrast, have encroached upon routine action.

In this context, particular types of reflexive negotiation of social contexts allow the possibility for new forms of social mobilisations to emerge and for new transnational networks and movements to articulate effectively demands for social change. The chapter will examine specifically the newly emerged youth-led *School Strike for Climate* movement.[1] The

---

[1] The global movement inspired by Greta Thunberg is known among other names as 'Fridays for Future' (FFF), 'Youth Strike for Climate', 'Global Strike for Climate' or 'Strike for Climate' and has an online presence under such names both as websites and as social media groups (with their local versions). For the purpose of consistency, I will refer to this as the School Strike for Climate in order to stay close to the

argument advanced here is that phenomena such as these need to be understood in terms of connecting the micro-level of individual reflexive situatedness in the world with the macro-level of the social order, via the meso-level of social networks. This entails exploring the capacity the former has, in specific contexts, to disrupt existing structures and to exert transformative pressures on society. This is done by placing reflexivity, and more specifically meta-reflexivity and its relational function in mediating structure, agency and culture interaction at the centre of explaining social dynamics. It uses the case of environmental activist Greta Thunberg and her role in fomenting the basis for a global climate action protest movement.

Implicitly at least, explorations (discussed later on) of the increased role of reflexivity at the expense of habitual action and the accentuation of morphogenetic processes at the expense of morphostatic ones beg for a further theoretical question regarding whether – in broader terms – we are witnessing a shift to a new kind of social formation: a morphogenic society. It is beyond the intentions of this chapter to make any claims about the advance or impending coming of a morphogenic society. Such ideas are currently being posited – in an exploratory way and with appropriate qualifications – in a series of studies that brings together scholars who operate from both within and outside critical realism.[2] The point made here (incidentally) is that the inquiries into the possible advent of a morphogenic society are useful in providing a circumscribing scope for understanding emergent social movements that have a transformative potential in relation to social structures and the social order.

Thus, this chapter starts by presenting the key features of the morphogenetic approach. It then sketches briefly the basis from which Archer and others are exploring the question of a nascent morphogenic society. This leads to a discussion about the increased role of reflexivity in late modernity, highlighting the conditions in which meta-reflexivity gains ground, and other modes of reflexivity become less prominent. Finally, the case of the *School Strike for Climate* is analysed looking at the relation between individual and collective reflexivity and paying attention to the cultural and structural contexts in which agents operate. The discussion

---

text Greta Thunberg – who was the spark behind this phenomenon – displayed on the strike banner.

[2] See the collective works edited by Archer 2013a, 2014a, 2015, 2016, 2017.

of the movement does not make normative claims about the nature of the values that inform action in this case. It is mainly concerned with identifying a satisfactory explanation for how such movements come into being; it explores in a specific context how structure, agency and culture, "each of which is relatively autonomous and possesses its own distinctive emergent properties and causal powers [...] simultaneously account for their combined elaboration [...and t]ogether they 'make history'" (Archer 2012: 5). The main concern of this edited collection points to global communities, and more specifically to how actors operate and how new types of transnational communities emerge in the current global(ising) context. Since the beginning of the twenty-first century we are seeing a proliferation of protest actions and movements that challenge deeply embedded structures and institutions and that are increasingly trans-national in their visibility and/or in their nature. These new trends are illustrated by the 2003 protests opposing the imminent war in Iraq, which involved coordinated actions by millions of people across a large number of countries; the Arab Spring revolution that started in Tunisia and spread throughout the region and led to regime changes in Tunisia, Egypt and Libya, as well as ongoing violence in Syria and Yemen; the post-financial-crisis Occupy movement against inequality and social injustice, starting in New York in 2011 and spreading to over eighty countries; the anti-racism Black Lives Matter movement started in 2013 by the killing of Trayvon Martin and re-fuelled recently by the killing of George Floyd; the *#Me Too* movement against sexual harassment and abuse that took off in 2017 after the public exposure of sexual abuse allegations against former film producer (and now, convicted sex offender) Harvey Weinstein; and the various groups and actions under the umbrella of climate change. In this context, the *School Strike for Climate* movement offers a suitable springboard for such inquiries. It is a relatively new phenomenon and it has the advantage of allowing a careful examination of structure-action-culture at the individual (reflexively mediated) level, as well as the collective one. As such, it provides scope for an empirical testing of the theoretical construction drawing on meta-reflexivity and morphogenesis.

Morphogenesis and nascent morphogenic society

Social changes that these movements are involved in are often summarised in an explanatory way under the label of globalisation. An umbrella term globalisation generally refers to processes of "shrinkage" or "compression" of the world or of space and time (Harvey 1991, Robertson 1992: 8, Larsson 2001: 9), an acceleration and intensification of social, political, economic and cultural relations (Giddens 1990: 64, Holm, Sørensen 1995: 12) and an increased awareness of these changes taking place (Robertson 1992: 8, Waters 1993:3). The issue with such perspectives on the current social world is – as Colin Wright (2014: 221–222) suggests – that they refer to globalisation as both a set of processes and as the effect of such processes. In addition to the quasi-conflation between process and outcomes, causal explanations[3] for what triggers these processes – even when a multitude of factors are considered – tend to only highlight tendencies, rather than explaining how such tendencies are activated. Put simply, they connect a set of processes (globalisation) with a set of factors of change (be they economic, social, technological, etc.) without a clear indication of how these are activated. In other words, agency is being dimmed out of this relational equation (Wright: 222). Another label attached to the current era is that of *network society*. For Manuel Castells, the technological revolution has led to an information age and to the reconfiguring of society into a new structure that is comprised of ever-expanding and reconfiguring powered networks interacting within a global system. In this new system, social morphology takes prominence over social action (Castells 2010: xviii, 500). He offers a convincing account of the use and flow of information, and of the powered interactions within and between networks. However, for Castells, rather than operating outside structure and agency or being mutually constitutive of structure and agency, social networks are social structures. In his view, the need to theorise social structures as interactive information networks stems from the fact that what he calls the four dimensions of the new society (technological, globalising, electronic and political) transform social structures into being much more adaptive, flexible, able to expand and reconfigure themselves, making them more resilient (Castells, 2008). By focusing on the macro-level, however, it appears that in his account, too, agency ends up somewhat collapsed into the structure, embedded into the power-driven interactions between networks. He

---

[3] Held, McGrew, Goldblatt and Perraton (1999: 12) summarise the approaches to what drives globalisation processes by distinguishing between monocausal (and thus reductionist) explanations (largely focusing on market capitalist forces) and more complex ones that point to the intersection of a multiplicity of forces that include economic, technological, social and political change.

nuances this position slightly in the second volume of his trilogy on the network society by emphasising the transformational powers of *project identities*, that may emerge out of *resistance identities*,[4] and pursue the values of communal resistance against global flows (Castells 2009: 421). Still, agency in this framework is only visible at the level of the collective. At the micro-level, his approach does not account for individual agency and its role in forming collective engagement with the new structures. More importantly, at a broad level, he remains more or less descriptive of processes and effects that take place in the context of this new social reality (the network society), as it does not identify how these processes come about and what their generative mechanisms are (Archer 2014b: 103).

By contrast, the morphogenetic approach allows the possibility for an investigation that rests on a stratified social ontology that is concerned with how things work, accounts for the analytical distinction between the material, the agential and the ideational (or structure, agency and culture – SAC), and unpacks their interaction chronologically. A M/M cycle can be summarised in a number of propositions claiming that:

- Structure, agency and culture are analytically distinct and irreducible to one another;
- Structure and culture pre-date agency;
- The M/M cycle captures the interaction in the structural domain between structure and agency (social interaction) and in the cultural domain between culture and agency (socio-cultural interaction), as well as the feedback between them;
- The interaction may result, respectively, in structural or cultural elaboration (morphogenesis) or in the existing structure or culture being reinforced (morphostasis) (Archer 1995, Archer 2013b: 7 Figure 1.1 and Figure 1.2).

In other words, when exploring any "slice" of social reality, time has to be accounted for in mapping out relational dynamics. Thus, the starting point (T1) is one of conditioning by pre-existing structures and culture (each with autonomous causal properties). The second phase involves agency interaction over time with the enablements and constraints exerted by structure and culture (T2–T3). The final phase in the cycle (T4) represents the

---

4   Resistance identities are communal entities built around 'people resisting economic, cultural and political disfranchisement' and they may remain at the level of a 'defensive commune' or evolve into project identities (Castells 2009: 421–422).

outcome of the interaction which may be morphogenesis or morphostasis. Social change can be accounted for and explained by closely monitoring the interaction taking place within these cycles (Archer 1995: 76–79).

The debates from within the morphogenetic approach camp (and not only) concerning the rapidity with which social change occurs in late modernity has recently expanded to incorporate questions on whether we are now witnessing a potential shift to a morphogenetic society. This overall line of investigation starts from the observation that over the last few decades, we have seen an acceleration of the pace at which social change takes place. As Maccarini suggests, "late modern society faces the continuous need to question its own foundations, which results in the endemic 'crisis' of most institutions, identities, *habitus*, and forms of individual and collective action in their 'modern' configuration" (2014: 49). In this context, structural and cultural conditionings offer a wider range of possibilities for actions by individuals and collectives, a situation – as Archer has repeatedly put it – of variety producing more variety (Archer 2014, Maccarini 2014: 49). Technological development, and in particular the rise of high-speed Internet and of multi-actor flows of information (which have escaped the control of the state) are increasingly enabling dissent and supporting the articulation of protest as well as the organisation of social action. These aspects are highlighted in detail by Castells (2015) in his examination of protest movements. What the focus on morphogenesis (and the possible advent of a morphogenic society) does is to provide an explanatory framework for these changes. Simply drawing a causal relationship between the development of new technology and events and movements such as the Arab Spring, Occupy, etc., that have captured the interest of researchers does not allow us to explain such social dynamics properly. New technology itself only represents an enabling mechanism that these new networks and structures display, rather than a causal mechanism that explains social change (Wright 2014: 57). The explanatory power comes out of the exploration of the interaction between structure, agency and culture, at the level of both the individual and the collective, with reflexivity acting as the relational element in this process.

Reflexivity and the role of meta-reflexives in social change

The morphogenic approach employed in the present chapter highlights the importance of considering structure, agency and culture as analytically distinct and of explaining social change or status quo on the basis of the interaction between these, over time. In other words, we are neither complete masters of our destiny, nor are we fully determined by the (material and ideational) contexts in which we operate. Instead, through our internal conversations, we make sense of the work around us (the structural and cultural conditioning) from the perspective of our ultimate concerns, and on that basis, derive life strategies and act upon them.[5] In Archer's conception, reflexivity refers to "the regular exercise of the mental ability, shared by all normal people, to consider themselves in relation to their (social) contexts and vice versa", and it offers an answer to how its subjective power mediates the "role that objective structural or cultural powers play in influencing social action" (Archer 2007: 4–5). Reflexivity is, thus, the key to explaining SAC interaction. On this basis, Archer opposes dominant positions in current social theory (occupied by Pierre Bourdieu and Ulrich Beck) that engage with reflexivity as a way to account for the crises bought about by late modernity. For Bourdieu, reflexivity is accounted for as a playing a secondary role, with the habitus – as embedded pre-conscious actions, values or dispositions – situated at the forefront. In addition, he sees habitus as a system of internalised structures that is common to all members of a group (Bourdieu 1977: 86). Archer contends that Bourdieu's engagement with reflexivity suffers from elisionism (or central conflation) because in his view agency and structure are not ontologically and analytically distinct. In addition, the emphasis on routine action suggests a high propensity for the reproduction of existing social structures (morphostasis), thus not accounting adequately for social transformation. Beck's articulation of the reflexive modernity is better suited to account for the decline of routine action in late modernity, but conceives reflexivity largely as a process operating at the societal level, and not at that of individual agents; and – linked to that – maintains a central-conflationist approach, that does not allow for an analysis of the interaction between structure and agency (Archer 2007: 29–37, Chernilo 2017: Ch.7).[6]

---

[5]   It is through reference to the mediation of cultural and structural conditions via internal conversation that we are able to explain why individuals facing exactly the same circumstances may act in very different ways.

[6]   Another important criticism directed at Beck's reflexive modernity theory is the fact that it suggests that reflexivity is a feature of late modernity alone, forced upon individuals by the conditions of risk and uncertainty that were not visible in traditional societies. By contrast, Archer maintains that reflexivity is indispensable to

Archer proposes a reflexivity model that entails several features. First, it distinguishes between four different reflexive modes that individuals display in their internal conversations, and which mediate the way in which people make sense of their social-cultural context and derive courses of action based on their personal projects. *Communicative reflexives* require that others (normally their social circle of "similars and familiars") provide an external validation for their internal conversation, before that can lead to action. By contrast, *autonomous reflexives* are self-sufficient, and their internal deliberations lead directly to action. For *meta-reflexives* the internal conversation is not limited to being action-oriented. They reflect critically on their own internal conversations, on their actions, and on their impact on society. The final (residual) category comprises the *fractured reflexives* whose internal conversations end up in a loop, unable to derive purposeful courses of action, which, in turn, leads to an intensification of distress and disorientation (Archer 2007: 93). Second, it has to be noted that articulated in this way, these reflexive modes are ideal types. Individuals are likely to display all/most of these modes in their daily social interactions. While the reflexive process is a heterogeneous, multi-faceted one, individuals develop a dominant mode in the way they engage with contexts and situations and deliberate on them. Finally, the reflexive process can be unpacked into a dialectical sequence of *concerns* → *projects* → *practices*. This starts with the individual assessing the context in which they are situated in terms of "defining and dovetailing concerns" and prioritising among them, leading to articulating concrete courses of action and finally establishing a *modus vivendi* (with sustainable practices) out of these projects (Archer 2007: 88–89).

More recently, Archer's preoccupation has been to explore more thoroughly the connection between the increased prevalence of morphogenesis, at the expense of morphostasis (i.e. faster pace of social change) and reflexivity. A number of observations that can guide the exploration into the *School Strike for Climate* movement emerge from this. First of all, increased morphogenesis renders the individual in a situation of "contextual incongruity" where past guidelines and routine action do not offer appropriate information to deal with novel, diverse and unpredictable

---

any society (whether traditional, modern or late-modern). As she puts it: 'no reflexivity; no society' (Archer 2007: 25–33).

situations; the latter increasingly require reflexive deliberations – what Archer (2012) has labelled the "reflexive imperative". The second refers to the first phase of the reflexive sequence: concerns are shaped and prioritised on the basis of the context in which the individual is situated. Faced with "contextual incongruity" of changeable contexts, personal concerns play an increasing role in how projects and practices are articulated (Archer 2012: 6, 42–43). It is important to bear in mind at this point that at a basic level, human choice is divided between self-interest and morality. The former entails egotistic concerns (about one's individual well-being or – by extension – the well-being of those close to them), while the latter refers to what is right, irrespective of the impact on the reflexive individual. However, the exercise of free will is a mechanism that does not operate in a vacuum. As suggested earlier, we are not full masters of our destiny; our agency is exercised within the contingencies of the existing structural/material and cultural/ideational enablements an constrains (Porpora 2015: 192).[7] With this in mind, the third observation refers to the fact that nascent morphogenesis does not only impact on reflexivity in a quantitative way through the intensification in reflective practice and a decline of habitual action. There is also a qualitative change of modality: meta-reflexivity is moving to a position of dominance (Maccarini 2013: 40, Archer 2014b: 111). To put it simply, "faster morphogenesis introduces a completely unprecedented influence of structure and culture upon personal reflexivity, which promotes a distinctive mode of reflexive deliberation – meta-reflexivity" (Archer 2012: 31–32). This is so because, with more relevance given to personal concerns than to fast-changing contexts, self-critique becomes crucial to developing courses of action. In turn, the viability of personal projects in the outer world becomes more and more predicated on social critique. These factors, coupled with structural developments that entail the development and diversification of the third sector, provide opportunities for many individuals to pursue their value commitments, that is to develop a sustainable practices (Archer 2012: 43–45). Attempting a sketched portrait of the emerging young generation of meta-reflexives, Archer observes the paradoxical features of the " 'loners' who seek to devote themselves to social relations" and who are "critically detached from that part of the social order they know best yet dedicated to re-ordering the social

---

[7]   As Porpora remarks, the distinction between self-interest and moral concerns does not mean that they are necessarily mutually conflicting or exclusive (2015: 192).

through their vocational endeavours" (2012: 210). Finally, technological developments remove the individuals' ties to specific locations and act as enablers for nimbler, less structured forms of community organisation. Coupled with the rise of meta-reflexivity, this results in the rise of new forms of collective agency promoting new interests and formulating new ways to advance them (Archer 2012: 31, Lawson 2014: 28).

The case of the *School Strike for Climate* movement

The previous sections aimed to draw on the morphogenetic approach as a meta-theory as a platform for selecting theoretical tools that provide an explanatory frame for understanding how global communities form in the current phase of modernity. This is tested empirically in the next section, through looking at the dynamics that led to the emergence and development of the *School Strike for Climate* movement. To sum up, this chapter argues that to make sense of this movement, a SAC examination is necessary as a way to analytically unpick how emergent properties associated with each of the SAC components are being activated through their interaction. At the level of agency, late modern society (and potentially nascent morphogenic society) has resulted in emerging synergies between structure and culture that generate an acceleration of morphogenesis, which in turn has led to increased reflexivity and a decline of routine action. Moreover, it is a particular mode of reflexivity – metareflexivity – that seems to gain ground, at the expense of the other three. The dominance of this type of reflexive mediation of structure and culture increasingly allows for projects that are critical of the current social order and aim to change it to emerge and to find novel solutions for social mobilisation and action.

Consequently, this section will start with a brief account of how the movement developed and gained ground. It will then explore the question of agency starting from the level of the individual (primary) agent, with a particular focus on Greta Thunberg – the catalyst for the movement – to the transformative formation of collective (corporate agency). The cultural paradigm in which the debates about climate change occur will be briefly outlined, then followed by a discussion of the structural entablements and constraints. Inevitably, the analysis will only be sketched as a way to illustrate empirically the theoretical claims relating to morphogenesis and (meta-)reflexivity. After all, this exploration starts from the premises that (social) reality is stratified and SAC causal properties and interaction may constitute new structures new causal properties that are different from the parts in the stratum below and their aggregation. Thus, the analysis will only pick up on a number of SAC components, without assuming that they are the only ones exerting causal efficacy or that they operate in a vacuum.

Context

On 20 August 2018, Greta Thunberg, a young Swedish girl, then fifteen, started a one-person protest in front of the Swedish Parliament. Prompted by the wave of wild fires and drought in Sweden that year, she held a sign that said *School Strike for Climate* (*Skolstrejk för klimatet* in Swedish), and committed to strike from school until the general elections due on the 9th of September that year, demanding tougher government action on combatting climate change (Crouch 2018). Over the following days, other people joined her strike, and soon one young girl's act went viral and acted as a catalyst for a growing youth movement opting for direct action in order to secure social and political changes in relations to what has been labelled as the current climate emergency. The social movement developed as a broad umbrella for a wide range of individuals and organisations, and operates as a broad network of nodal groups with loose organisational structure and quasi-autonomy in organising and coordinating activities locally. As a result, since 2018, this movement has grown and is characterised by scale, geographical coverage and sustained activities. For example, between the end of 2018 and the beginning of 2020, the FFF website mapped up strikes taking place in over 160 countries (involving over four million people) at the peak of the period, stabilising towards the end of the timeframe at over 140 counties (but with very small numbers of participants) (see Tab. 1).

In addition to snowballing its own success, the movement and its initiator have had an important contribution in giving impetus to other groups sharing similar concerns and targeting similar outcomes. For instance, the youth action has inspired the older generation into action, with equivalent Parents against Climate Change groups organising. More importantly, other organisations, such as the Extinction Rebellion (XR) – established earlier in 2018, were spurred into direct action, against the background of the prominence of the climate emergency debates generated by Thunberg's actions. The XR engaged in protest blockades, site occupations and civil disobedience activities in London

Tab. 1. Source: Fridays for future 2020a.

Country\Date	30 Nov	15 Feb	15 Mar	3 May	24 May	21 Jun	20 Sep	27 Sep	29 Nov	6 Dec	13 Dec	10 Jan	17 Jan	24 Jan	31 Jan	7 Feb	14 Feb
#Countries	17	31	135	78	131	98	167	163	156	144	142	141	143	143	143	143	144
#Cities	287	233	2370	603	1976	649	3972	2381	2419	1561	1458	1461	1480	1477	1482	1488	1518
#Events	294	270	2613	730	2372	836	4716	3237	3398	2443	2283	2294	2317	2314	2332	2342	2390
#People	26493	10505	2289750	40401	751649	60219	4031255	3761485	1199065	523323	56804	1873	2978	760	401	837	6648

towards the end of 2018 and such activities expanding to North America and Australia at the beginning of 2019.[8]

Primary agency and moral grounding

The case of Greta Thunberg presents an interesting empirical illustration of meta-reflexivity in action. The public development of this case provides access to observing how individual internal conversations play out in the social world. The first aspect indicating the dominance of the meta-reflexive mode in the case of Greta Thunberg concerns her critical positioning assumed with regards to the self and to her immediate and wider social interactions. Numerous accounts drawn from her own public statements and biographical details coming from her parents showcase, on the one hand, the difficulties in engaging in meaningful social interactions with her peers and the detachment from her most proximate social bonds (the family), and on the other hand, the critical evaluation of her own internal conversations in terms of formulating and endorsing personal projects as well as the value-oriented nature of this process (Archer 2007: 300–303, Archer 2012, 2010). Greta, herself spoke about her sense of social inadequacy, positioning herself in contradistinction with what is socially perceived as "normality": "I was too bad at socialising, I just hated making small talk and constantly being around so many people" (Rowlatt 2020). Having been diagnosed with Asperger's syndrome (which prior to the diagnosis had led her to eating disorders, depression and serious health concerns, as well as to further social marginalisation in school),[9] Greta Thunberg has embraced her situation often referring to it as a "gift" or a "superpower" which has helped her articulate her commitment to the climate emergency cause:

> Some people mock me for my diagnosis. But Asperger is not a disease, it's a gift. People also say that since I have Asperger I couldn't possibly have put

---

[8] Some of the XR actions in the UK led the counter-terrorism police placing the group on a list of extremist organisations and to issuing guidance about it with regards to safeguarding young people against extremist ideologies. The guidance was later recalled, and officials stated publicly that they did not con-sider XR to be an extremist organisation (Dodd and Grierson 2020).

[9] A detailed account of Greta Thunberg's health struggles and how they led to shaping her values and actions in relation to climate change comes from her parents (see Thunberg et al. 2020).

myself in this position. But that's exactly why I did this. Because if I would have been "normal" and social I would have organised myself in an organisation, or started an organisation by myself (Thunberg 2019: 30).

The lack of resonance with and distancing from the family social bonds or the critique of the values and social goods available within that environment – a characteristic of meta-reflexivity -- is expressed by Thunberg in unequivocal terms: "It felt like I was the only one who cared about the climate and the ecological crisis [...] My parents didn't care about it, my classmates didn't care about it, my relatives didn't care about this" (Rowlatt 2020).

Her reflexive sequence of *concerns – practices – projects* is guided by a conflict between the self-interest and ethical concerns, with the latter taking primacy over the former, the moral drive then shaping projects, which in turn, are dedicating to "re-ordering the social through [...] vocational endeavours" (Archer 2012: 210). In personal terms, this is illustrated by her choice to become vegan and to stop flying as a way to "walk the talk" and to exert influence on her parents to follow that example (even though they confessed to changing their lifestyle for her sake rather than for the cause she is pursuing) (Dolsak, Prakash 2019, Thunberg 2019: 5). In terms of the broader exercise of agency, she has been able to subvert and disrupt existing morphostatic structures and agents. Her strong public profile and popularity have enabled her to exert powerful agential emergent properties by galvanising collective support for the climate emergency struggle, shaping the organisation of a global community of like-minded agents and setting the tone and agendas for global summits and enhancing a counter-narrative to other strong agents advocating status quo in terms of environment protection of articulating climate-denial narratives.[10] While there is no scope for wider generalisation on the role of individual meta-reflexivity in shaping collective action and social change based on a single (albeit very relevant) case, existing research on climate change offers further evidence for the dominance of meta-reflexivity in generating morally-informed social practices. Empirical research by Davidson

---

[10] There are numerous examples in this respect: setting the ground for the School Strike for Climate movement, speaking a various climate marches, pro-tests and actions, speaking at international for a such as the UN Climate Change Conference in Poland, in 2018, at the World Economic Forum in Davos in 2019, at the European Economic and Social Committee in Brussels, in 2019, at the European Parliament in Strasbourg, in 2019, etc. (Thunberg 2019).

and Stedman on reflexivity and climate change attitudes based on over 1000 respondents shows "a strong association between Meta-Reflexivity and willingness to engage in climate-related behaviours" (2018: 80).

At the very least this discussion on primary agency and meta-reflexivity in relation to climate change movements shows a propensity of these actors to derive courses of action based primarily on concerns that are *deontic* rather than *aretaic* in nature (Porpora 2015: 192). In the right conditions (as the Greta Thunberg case shows), individual agency has the power to exert significant morphogenic force: when agents activate their causal powers and confront structures that are incongruent with their *modus vivendi,* the interaction can result in the elaboration of new structures (Archer 1995). Causally, however, this has to be understood relationally, in terms of its interaction with other structures, culture and other agents.

Corporate agency and social action

So far, I have discussed the case of Greta Thunberg as a catalyst for climate justice action. This has been explained through the propensity of meta-reflexives to pursue value-based personal projects. As a next step to make sense of how the *School Strike for Climate* emerged as a global collective that exerts its own causal powers (operating in the context of the stratified social reality at a level above that of individual agency) it is important to differentiate between primary agency and corporate agency involved in the SAC interaction and capable of change in the area of climate emergency. In simple terms, individuals and collectivities exert causal powers, these powers are – due to a lack of organisation and strategic pursuit of interests – less effective in initiating social change. Corporate agents – as Archer puts it – "pack more punch in defining and re-defining structural forms" (Archer 1995: 190–191). As such, the impact of private agency on society is merely expressed as an aggregate at best. Mobilisation of primary agents into corporate ones enables agency to operate at a different level and exert more influence on structure. Here, again, the nature of late modernity and dominance of meta-reflexivity provide a context in which transformation of primary agency into new forms of corporate agency is possible, with organised groups drawn more towards social justice and the third sector (which provide increase attraction in terms of reflecting the value commitments of meta-reflexives) and articulating aims on a global scale (Archer 2007: 313, Archer 2012: 45).

In the social-political realm corporate agency during modernity has largely been organised alongside the state and the market (with a particular dependency on electoral politics structures). Thus, collective interests have been articulated alongside political parties, unionised worker groups, and employer groups.[11] Late modernity has given way increasingly to political engagement and the coagulation of interest groups that are active outside the electoral politics and display novel forms of interaction. Climate change action and the *School Strike for Climate* movement specifically fall in this latter category. The transformation of agency from primary into corporate involves a morphogenic process that develops over time, starting (as with any morphogenic process as articulated in Archer's approach) with a T1 moment of socio-cultural conditioning of groups, a T2–T3 process of interaction and a T4 moment of group elaboration (Archer 1995: 194).

Following this process in the case the *School Strike for Climate*, the T1 moment is characterised by contingent compatibilities (specific structural and cultural configurations to be outlined later) which provide the context for primary agency interaction. The engine for this interaction was, here, the strike action initiated by Greta Thunberg on the 20th of August 2018. Soon after, several other fellow students, teachers and parents joined her at her spot in front of the Swedish Parliament. Widespread social media coverage shot the profile of the direct action sky-high, giving it global exposure and sparking similar school walk-outs among school children with 17,000 students organising strikes in 24 countries by September, the same year (Gould 2019). This stage of interaction takes the shape social protests spreading across the world designating Fridays (following Thunberg's example) as days of action. This corresponds to an aggregation of primary agency and further mobilisation and organisation results in corporate agency taking shape, with the *Fridays for Future* movement establishing its Internet presence, gaining more coherence in organising protests, and stating demands (see Fig. 1).[12] Related groups, such as the

---

[11] These agents were able to operate within states as well as (with increased globalisation) in the international realm (through inter-governmental organisations, trans- and multi-national corporations, etc.).

[12] Their August 2019 'Declaration of Lausanne' names keeping the global temperature rise under 1.5 degrees Celsius, ensuring climate justice and equity, and drawing on scientific consensus as their key demands (Fridays for Future 2020b). The group defines itself as a global movement and claims its birth to be the day Greta Thunberg started her strike. Despite the fact that the claim blurs the different moments

Global Climate Strike, follow the same pattern of organisation. They operate at a different level (meso-level) than the aggregation of primary agency because of their capacity to articulate their collective interest, are organised and "can engage in concerted action" (Archer 1995: 258).

Enabling cultural factors

As discussed, culture as a key element of the SAC interaction plays an important role in the conditioning taking place at the T1 moment of the M/M process. It comes with its own set of enablements and constraints that are reflexively mediated by agents via internal conversation, and that influence outcome. As the overall purpose of this chapter is to explore how new global communities of action emerge in late modernity, the focus would be on the elements that are more conducive to morphogenesis. In the case of the *School Strike for Climate* movement, agent action (from both the primary and the corporate circles) takes place against a particular set of growing dominant cultural frames relating to climate change. There is, in other words an increasingly visible culture of environmental concern.

This context can be summarised by referring to several inter-connected factors visible during late modernity. To begin with, environmental concerns have been on the political agenda since the 1960s and have become an increasingly salient aspect of political debates. This has happened through the growing number of green parties being established, entering competition for power and gaining parliamentary representation.[13] Such developments also led to an indirect effect of "greening" of established parties (Carter 2007). To put it simply, the environmental issue has gone mainstream: it is quasi-impossible for a contemporary political party not to have an official position (whatever that may be) with regards to the environment. In parallel, there has been a consolidation of the relevance of the environment as a political issue especially in the developed world. The most recent Eurobarometer Survey, for instance, shows that 94 per cent of EU citizens stated that the protection of the environment was important to them, 91 per cent thought that climate change was a serious concern and 83 per cent felt the necessity for European legislation to target environment

---

in the articulation of the movement, the difference between the aggregation of primary agencies and the emergent corporate agency is analytically important for unpacking the process.

[13] Looking at the electoral performance of green parties in Europe, Carter shows a visible pattern of success since their emergence (Carter 2007: 89, Table 4.1).

protection (European Commission 2020). Finally, growing evidence has led to the emergence of a consensus among the scientific community with regards to the anthropogenic nature of climate change. A claim that has been widely circulated in the academic literature and among various political figures is that of a 97 per cent consensus on the human-driven climate change.[14] Whether or not the 97 per cent figure is accurate, there is widespread recognition that a majority of the scientific community is positioned within the anthropogenic paradigm (Ritchie 2016, Tol 2016).

The narrative scientific consensus on climate change represents a powerful opportunity provided by the cultural system. Indeed, it has been treated as such by the agents involved in climate change mobilisation. At the individual level, Greta Thunberg has repeatedly made reference to her reliance, in her speeches, on the evidence coming from the scientific community, urging politicians to "talk to scientists" and to "listen to them", to act on predictions that are "backed by scientific facts" coming from the Intergovernmental Panel on Climate Change (IPCC) and remarking that "every major scientific body around the world unreservedly supports the [...] findings of the IPCC" (Thunberg 2019: 38, 50–51). The official FFF website also makes ample reference to the scientific discourse and evidence on climate change as a way to both justify their action and articulate demands (FFF 2020).

Structures of opportunity

The final element in the SAC interaction concerns the structural context within which agency operates in the case of the *School Strike for Climate*. It is suggested here that specific contingent opportunities have contributed to the emergence of the movement as a global community of organised action.

The first set of enabling structures that help to explain this new form of social organisation is represented by the technology-aided networks within which primary agents interact. Thus, at the micro-level of social interaction, these networks emerge – as Castells (2008) argues – as new structures characteristic of what he calls *information society*.[15] However, the critical realist approach recognises the stratified

---

[14] This specific figure has been subjected to criticism from various camps, including those who recognise the human causes for climate decline (see Tol 2016).

[15] It is useful to point out here that Greta Thunberg was not the first young girl to speak publicly about the environment. In 1992, Severn Cullis-Suzuki, a 12-year-old

nature of social reality where "what appears as a structure at one level becomes an agent at another level" (Wright 2014: 225).[16] Earlier, I have outlined the corporate agential role that emerges out of the interaction at a micro-level of primary agents (with meta-reflexivity as a dominant mode), in their attempt to operationalise their value commitments. In that context, these networks of communication and interaction emerge at the meso-level as agents exerting a different kind of emergent properties, in a different stratum of social reality. The same networks act as structures at the lower (micro-)level. It is in recognising the potential dual nature of a social component, depending on which level of social reality it operates, that the M/M approach to explaining late modernity differs from the network approach proposed by Castells. In addition, the focus on technology and information only describes some of the enabling conditions visible in late modernity; it is necessary to look to deeper social processes and phenomena and interactions (Wright 2015: 57). In the context, it is important to point out that the interaction and aggregation of primary agency through these networks of communication have contributed to the process of organising social protests. Regular calls for strikes under the FFF "banner" have resulted in coordinated action across large numbers of countries and ultimately helps to explain the emergence of the *School Strike for Climate* global movement.

The other important phenomenon is the emergence over the last few decades, of several organisational and legal structures that provide further opportunities for climate change engagement. The United Nations Millennium Summit in 2000, for instance, included environmental sustainability as one of the eight key goals set up in the Millennium Development Goals (MDGs) framework, which committed all UN members to action. Its "heir", the Sustainable Development Goals framework, established in the 2015, has positioned the issue of sustainable environment at its core

---

Canadian girl and founder of the Environmental Children's Organisation spoke at the Earth Summit. Arguably, social media tools such (Instagram, Twitter, Facebook and YouTube) – not available in 1992 – contributed to the significantly higher impact of Thunberg's initiative (Han and Ahn 2020: 6).

[16] He exemplifies the different levels of analysis in the context of the international system where at a lower level, there is interaction between bureaucracies (as structures) and individuals (as agents), replaced at the level above by the nation state (as structure) and bureaucracies (as agents) and further above by the international system (as structure) and nation-states (as agents) (Wright 2014: 225).

(being embedded in goals such as "Health and Well-being", "Affordable and Clean Energy", "Sustainable Cities and Communities", etc., as well as being articulated in its own right, in the "Climate Action" goal) (UN [no date]). In a more focused way, the emphasis on climate change concerns at an international level has led – at the Rio de Janeiro Earth Summit in 1992 – to the setting up of the United Nations Framework Convention on Climate Change being founded.[17] From there, the Kyoto Protocol (in 1997) and the Paris Agreement (in 2015) set up mechanisms to opera-tionalise the framework (UNFCCC [n.d.]). All these structures, as well as emerging equivalent initiatives at regional and state level, provide a strong contextual basis for climate justice social actors to pursue interests and demands more effectively.

Morphostatic SAC

The unpacking of SAC interaction (related to climate change and the formation of global social movements) has highlighted that, in terms of enabling factors there exists an increased synchrony between culture and structure, which enables the liking between micro-level changes in reflexivity, meso-level transformations of networks and a potential macro-level re-articulation of the social order (Fig. 1).

These contingent compatibilities, in turn, create a new logic of oppor-tunity with morphogenic consequences (Archer 2013b: 1–21). This explanatory framework is used to analyse the emergence of a new type of meta-reflexive global community of action centred around climate justice.

Naturally, while this examination has focused primarily on the enabling properties in the agency, culture and structure, this does not mean that these are the only forces at play. Other actors, structures and cultural forms exert simultaneous competing morphostatic pressures and some will be briefly sketched below. At the individual level, peo-ple's values and commitments may be articulated differently than on a critical reflection on the human impact on the environment. Knowledge and ignorance play an important role in how people formulate projects.

---

[17]   The Framework entered into force in 1994 and set limits on greenhouse emissions for countries. However, these standards were non-binding and lacked enforcement mechanisms.

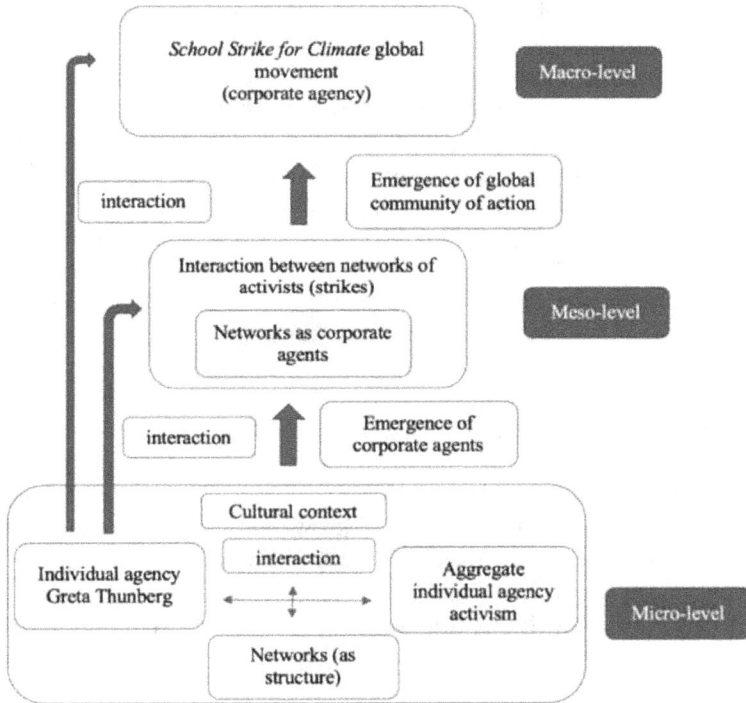

Fig. 1. Levels of agency interaction.

Self-interested concerns may take primacy over moral ones. Moral concerns can be articulated on different grounds than the environment. Last but not least, individuals have different levels of agency.[18] Corporate agents from within the market sphere can also exert strong pressures towards the *status quo*. Extractive industries and their lobbies, in particular, stand to be affected most by any stronger regulatory pressures on fossil fuel exploitation, and on carbon emissions, while other industries more broadly stand to lose from a more sustainable approach to consumerist issues. Finally, governments as actors in the international

---

[18] Moral choices in one's lifestyle are often determined by factors such as class, income, etc. For instance, it is likely that many people would be willing to consume ethically grown or organic food, but they are 'priced-out' and need to resort to food that is produced in more questionable ways.

arena can be vectors of morphostasis, as they need to aggregate the lower, national level, the interests of citizens, of businesses and of the third sector. Strong commitments to climate justice require significant expenditure that needs to be convincingly justified from an electoral perspective; thus, radical measures are unlikely. From the ideational register, a culture of individualism and consumerism characteristic of the neoliberal capitalist paradigm is undermining collective, social justice actions that threaten the status quo. Finally, the global power structures are still governed largely by the interplay between states and inter-governmental organisations on the one hand, and multi- and trans-national corporations, on the other. While the third sector has – as it has been argued here – increasingly opened avenues for the expression of values by those disenchanted with both the state and the market (Archer 2012: 44–45; 2014b: 111), this process is still in relatively early stages. Circumscribing all these aspects, the liberal capitalist system predicated on relations that "pit capitalist firms against each other in an ever-intensifying competition", and perpetual consumer-driven growth exerts the strongest morphostatic properties. A comprehensive approach to understanding social changes taking place at a particular moment in time would require the examination of all such of competing forces and their dynamic interactions over time.

By way of conclusion

This chapter has attempted to show how new global communities emerge and challenge existing structures. The *School Strike for Climate* case illustrates the increasing role meta-reflexivity plays in coalescing social movements and actions aiming at social change. This, in turn, hints at the need to engage more determinedly with the question concerning the advent of a morphogenetic society. However, this is not in any sense an argument that a tendency towards a morphogenic society is visible, nor is it a suggestion that such a tendency (if demonstrable) is likely to be, or ought to be activated. In fact, a quick look at the climate emergency movement's struggle to generate fundamental changes in how we – as humanity – operate in the world, so that to avoid climate calamity or extinction has so far failed. Despite the "noise" generated, extraction-based industries remain powerful agents that shape governmental agendas. By and large, individual choices are still driven by consumption. If anything, Trump's announcement in 2017 regarding the US withdrawal from the Paris Agreement,[19] and the looming post-Covid-19 pandemic economic recovery needs, indicate regress in terms of the attention that is likely to be given to climate protection measures. All these suggest that, so far, the movement has not been able to dislodge existing structures, and in this respect, morphostasis is the word of the day.

That being said, an important achievement lies first and foremost in the constitution of the movement itself. It indicates the increased influence meta-reflexivity has in generating a capacity for individual agents to coordinate alongside collective goals and engage in global action on that basis. As suggested earlier, this is not a unique occurrence in late modernity – with *Occupy* or *Black Lives Matter* movements operating on similar drivers. The proliferation of such types of actions is also telling of the increasingly morphogenic dimension of social interaction. Finally, and importantly, the *Strike for Climate* case shows an increase of the meta-reflexive mode through the fact that it prompted into action a demographic constituency that so far has not been particularly active in engaging in a struggle for social change. For once, some important changes are noticeable. First, the tone was given by young people under eighteen who managed to act as catalyst for a movement that drew into action a wide range of individuals and agents across the world. Second, they escalated the level of the public debate about climate change to one about climate emergency and – in the process – have raised important challenges to the *status quo*. They have done so by articulating demands in the name of the rights of the future generations, and by claiming political participation rights (e.g. lowering of the voting age to sixteen) on grounds of responsibility for the future. Enduring morphostatic factors (corporations, lobby groups, neoliberal capitalist consumerist culture and the capitalist system itself) notwithstanding, this research opens up a further hypothesis that is worth exploring: that some of the new social movements that we are witnessing have the capacity to be more salient and to live longer (thus strengthening their causal properties) because of the influence of meta-reflexivity has increased and because younger

---

[19] According to the terms of the Agreement, withdrawal is only possible three-year notice after the deal entered into force and another year notice for completion. This means that the US was officially projected to exit the Agreement on the 4th of November, one day after the elections (Farand 2019). However, one of the first executive orders passed by Joe Biden upon his election as US President was to return the US to the Paris Agreement.

people are more engaged with these movements. To put it differently, participants in these movements are being socialised in a more reflexive manner and in a context in which agency is interacting with culture and structure differently.[20]

References

Archer M.S., *Culture and Agency. The Place of Culture in Social Theory*, Cambridge, Cambridge University Press, 1988.

Archer M.S., *Realist Social Theory: The Morphogenetic Approach*, Cambridge, Cambridge University Press, 1995.

Archer M.S., *Being Human: The Problem of Agency*, Cambridge, Cambridge University Press, 2000.

Archer M.S., *Making Our Way through the World: Human Reflexivity and Social Mobility*, Cambridge, Cambridge University Press, 2007.

Archer M.S., *The Reflexive Imperative in Late Modernity*, Cambridge, Cambridge University Press, 2012.

Archer M.S., (ed.), *Social Morphogenesis*, Dordrecht, Springer, 2013a.

Archer M.S., "Social Morphogenesis and the Prospects of Morphogenic Society", in Archer M.S. (ed.), *Social Morphogenesis*, Dordrecht, Springer, 2013b, p. 1–22.

Archer M.S., (ed.), *Late Modernity. Trajectories Towards Morphogenic Society*, Dordrecht, Springer, 2014a.

Archer M.S., "The Generative Mechanism Re-configuring Late Modernity", in Archer M.S. (ed.), *Late Modernity. Trajectories Towards Morphogenic Society*, Dordrecht, Springer, 2014b, p. 93–117.

Archer M.S., (ed.), *Generative Mechanisms Transforming the Social Order*, Dordrecht, Springer, 2015.

Archer M.S., (ed.), *Morphogenesis and the Crisis of Normativity*, Dordrecht, Springer, 2016.

Archer M.S., (ed.), *Morphogenesis and Human Flourishing*, Dordrecht, Springer, 2017.

---

[20] I would like to thank my colleague, Dr Atsuko Ichijo, for drawing my attention to this particular direction for further research.

Carter N., *The Politics of the Environment. Ideas, Activism, Policy*, Cambridge, Cambridge University Press, 2007.

Castells M., "Materials for an Exploratory Theory of the Network Society", in *British Journal of Sociology*, no. 51(1), 2008, p. 5–24.

Castells M., *The Power of Identity. The Information Age: Economy, Society, and Culture*, Hoboken, Wiley-Blackwell, 2009.

Castells M., *The Rise of the Network Society*, Hoboken, Wiley-Blackwell, 2010.

Castells M., *Networks of Outrage and Hope: Social Movements in the Internet Age*, Cambridge, Polity, 2015.

Chernilo D., *Debating Humanity. Towards a Philosophical Society*, Cambridge, Cambridge University Press, 2017.

Crouch D., "The Swedish 15-Year-Old Who's Cutting Class to Fight the Climate Crisis", in *The Guardian*, 1 September 2018, https://www.theguardian.com/science/2018/sep/01/swedish-15-year-old-cutting-class-to-fight-the-climate-crisis.

Davidson D.J., Stedman R.C., "Calling Forth the Change-makers: Reflexivity Theory and Climate Change Attitudes and Behaviours", in *Acta Sociologica*, no. 61(1), 2018, p. 79–94.

Dodd V., Grierson J., "Terrorism Police List Extinction Rebellion as Extremist Ideology", in *The Guardian*, 10 January 2020, https://www.theguardian.com/uk-news/2020/jan/10/xr-extinction-rebellion-listed-extremist-ideology-police-prevent-scheme-guidance.

Dolsak N., Prakash A., "Does Great Thunberg's Lifestyle Equal Climate Denial? One Climate Scientist Seems to Suggest So", *Forbes*, 14 November 2019, https://www.forbes.com/sites/prakashdolsak/2019/11/14/does-greta-thunbergs-lifestyle-equal-climate-denial-one-climate-scientist-seems-to-suggest-so/#7c0a07ce67dc.

European Commission, "New Eurobarometer Survey: Protecting the Environment and Climate Is Important for over 90% of European Citizens", in *Press Release*, 3 March 2020, https://ec.europa.eu/commission/presscorner/detail/en/IP_20_331. Last viewed: 16 July 2020.

Farand C., "Trump Begins Formal US Withdrawal from Paris Agreement", in *Climate Home News*, 4 November 2019, https://www.climatechangenews.com/2019/11/04/trump-begins-formal-us-withdrawal-paris-agreement/.

Fridays for Future, "List of Countries", 16 July 2020a, https://fridaysforfuture.org/what-we-do/strike-statistics/list-of-countries/.

Fridays for Future, "Our Demands", 2020b, https://fridaysforfuture.org/what-we-do/our-demands/.

Giddens A., *The Consequences of Modernity*, Cambridge, Polity Press, 1990.

Gould L., "How Greta Thunberg's Climate Strikes Became a Global Movement in a Year", in *Reuters*, 20 August 2019, https://www.reuters.com/article/us-global-climate-thunberg/how-greta-thunbergs-climate-strikes-became-a-global-movement-in-a-year-idUSKCN1VA001.

Han H., Ahn S.W., "Youth Mobilization to Stop Global Climate Change: Narratives and Impact", in *Sustainability*, no. 12(10), 2020, p. 1–23.

Harvey D., *The Condition of Postmodernity. An Enquiry into the Origins of Cultural Change*, Cambridge Massachusetts, Blackwell, 1991.

Held D., McGrew A., Goldblatt D., Perraton J., *Global Transformations: Politics, Economics and Culture*, Stanford, Polity and Stanford University Press, 1999.

Holm H.H., Sørensen, G. (eds.), *Whose World Order? Uneven Globalization and the End of the Cold War*, Boulde, Westview Press, 2019.

Larsson T., *The Race to the Top: The Real Story of Globalization*, Washington, Cato Institute, 2001.

Larsson T., "A Speeding Up of the Rate of Social Change? Power, Technology, Resistance, Globalisation and the Good Society", in Archer M.S. (ed.), *Late Modernity. Trajectories Towards Morphogenic Society*, Dordrecht, Springer, 2014, p. 21–47.

Maccarini A., "The Emergent Social Qualities of a 'Morphogenic' Society: Cultures, Structures, and Forms of Reflexivity", in Archer M.S. (ed.), *Late Modernity. Trajectories Towards Morphogenic Society*, Dordrecht, Springer, 2014, p. 49–76.

Porpora D.V., "Why Don't Things Change? The Matter of Morphostasis", in Archer M.S. (ed.), *Generative Mechanisms Transforming the Social Order*, Dordrecht, Springer, 2015, p. 183–203.

Ritchie E.J., "Fact Checking the Claim of 97% Consensus on Anthropogenic Climate Change", in *Forbes*, 14 December 2016, https://www.forbes.com/sites/uhenergy/2016/12/14/fact-checking-the-97-consensus-on-anthropogenic-climate-change/#49d0a5d71157.

Robertson R., *Globalization: Social Theory and Global Culture*, London, Sage, 1992.

Rowlatt J., "Greta Thunberg, the Climate Campaigner Who Doesn't Like Campaigning", in *BBC News*, 4 July 2020, https://www.bbc.co.uk/news/stories-53255535?intlink_from_url=https://www.bbc.co.uk/news/topics/cwmrxq94v1jt/greta-thunberg&link_location=live-reporting-correspondent.

Thunberg G., *No One Is Too Small*, London, Penguin Books, 2019.

Thunberg G., Thunberg S., Ernman M., Ernman B., *Our House Is on Fire. Scenes of a Family and Planet in Crisis*, London, Penguin Books, 2020.

Tol R.S.J., "Comment on 'Quantifying the Consensus on Anthropogenic Global Warming in the Scientific Literature'", in *Environmental Research Letters*, no. 11(4), 2016, p. 1–6.

United Nations, "Sustainable Development", Department of Economic and Social Affairs, https://sdgs.un.org/goals [n.d.].

United Nations Framework Convention on Climate Change, "UNFCCC Process and Meetings", https://unfccc.int/process-and-meetings [n.d.].

Waters M., *Globalization*, London, Routledge, 1995.

Wright C., "Morphogenesis and Cooperation in the International Political System", in Archer M.S. (ed.), *Late Modernity. Trajectories Towards Morphogenic Society*, Dordrecht, Springer, 2014, p. 221–240.

Wright C., "Mechanisms and Models: Some Examples from International Relations", in Archer M.S. (ed.), *Generative Mechanisms Transforming the Social Order*, Dordrecht, Springer, 2015, p. 49–64.

The emergence of a smart global community. Zooms in and out from Miyako (Japan)

Fabienne Martin

In the Okinawa Prefecture of Japan, the small island of Miyako (Miyakojima) has been working for several years on the construction of a *smart* community: a new kind of community, both technical and multi-species, which connects multiple entities with distinct ontological statuses – humans, plants, animals, natural elements, objects, artefacts – by means of information and communication technologies, in order to respond to the problems associated with what one might call, for the sake of brevity, the anthropocene. The creation of such a community is not unique to Miyako, but is emerging all over the world, although the most advanced developments are to be found in Asia, particularly East Asia.

It is this new formulation of community, produced by a worrying environmental situation and based upon a technologisation of existence, which I propose to examine here, using an ethnographic study carried out on the island[1]. By alternating close-up views and enlarged views, I would like to show how the smart community that is being promoted in this Japanese island of Miyako partakes of, and is a part of, a larger whole that is unfolding on a planetary scale. In other words, I would like to show how this sited community constitutes *one* of the multiple parts of a larger world commanded by new technologies, that I propose to call the "smart global community", on which the smart community of Miyako depends, both in its present formulation and its form to come.

I would like to argue that what is at stake with the smart global community is a completely different kind of globalisation from the one we have known hitherto, and that what is emerging is a technological

---

[1] The city of Miyako is made up of six islands: five of them are connected by bridge and the sixth is uninhabited. It is this set that is meant by "Miyako island".

globalisation, which creates a "community" on a planetary scale, a non-territorialised community, with no major centre, driven by the techno-logical *functioning* and paradigmatic of a world that is taking shape.

Close-up

Where are we? On the world map, Miyakojima is a tiny dot lost in the blue of the ocean. It is necessary to zoom in to see appearing, in the China Sea, closer to the Taiwanese coast than to Tokyo two thousand kilometres away, this small triangular-shaping island; at the most, about thirty kilometres from west to east and north to south. The island is inhabited by about fifty-five thousand human beings, apart from the seasonal influx of tourists, mainly Japanese metropolitans, who come here to revel in the peaceful rhythm of life, the beauty of the beaches and outdoor recreation (diving, snorkelling, paddling, golf...). Tourism, along with the industry of sugarcane that is the major crop on the island, are the island's main sources of income, in addition to fishing, market gardening and forestry. Miyako likes to describe itself as a sunbathed island, home of beautiful nature and traditional culture.

But this little paradise also has its problems. The whole island is generally flat, having no mountains or rivers and has to tap groundwater for its water supply; daily life is highly dependant on food and energy resources from outside the island; its industry is in decline; its population is aging; and it is periodically hit by severe typhoons.

Yet all that does not prevent the island from having great ambitions for itself, for Japan and even for the world. The municipality of Miyako has indeed decided to embark on the construction of a *smart* community, which it describes as an unprecedented attempt to become a model of life for all secluded islands in Japan and throughout the globe. And we could add beyond that, as a model and almost a modelling of ecological microsystems that are to come.

It must be said that the smart community promises great things. These include: making the future beautiful with home-made energy; enabling local production for local consumption; providing food safety and job security; addressing the problems linked to the aging population; making a system for citizens to work together in close collaboration; generating wealth without destroying the planet; fighting climate change; or creating a rich environment where people never get tired of living. In sum, in the words of the Toshiba Company, which is deeply involved in the building of the smart community in Miyako, the aim is "to create an ideal human smart community, where people live in peace, safety, and comfort" (Toshiba Review 2015: 1).

Even closer view: Miyako smart community

How does this *smart* community operate in practice? It seems to begin with a human commitment, as shown by the *declaration* issued by the municipality of Miyako, which proclaims: "we [i.e. the whole human population of the island] will protect our precious ground water which supports the island's life. We will protect our beautiful corals reefs and the sea. We will conserve our limited resources and energy by using our wisdom and creativity. We will act individually, aiming to make Miyakojima beautiful, tidy, and earth [sic] friendly. We will think and act together with the peoples of the world to preserve and protect our environment and pass it on to future generations. We will protect our forests, sea, and air and act to make an environment in which all living things can co-exist" (Miyakojima City 2008).

Far from being limited to human beings, the concept of smart community implies a reconfiguration of the relationships between a multitude of existing ones. Like any *smart* community, that of Miyako is indeed a hybrid assemblage of beings of different "natures". Within the Miyako smart community we find in particular: a) sugarcane plants; b) fish; c) algae; d) microorganisms; e) humans; f) wind turbines erected on the northern and south-eastern capes of the island; g) solar panels by the tens of thousands, nestling on the roofs of schools, houses, administrative buildings, on the tops of cliffs and in the hollows of fields; h) photovoltaic power plants; i) storage batteries; j) small electric cars; k) charging stations; l) wind; m) rain; n) sunlight; o) the island's mascot character, a great defender of nature, with her blue hair in the shape of waves and foliage on her head; p) her sidekick, the energy superhero, in a golden suit and silver cape; q) refineries; r) eco-houses; s) waste; t) measuring devices; u) servers; v) software; w) data; x) a mangrove; y) a huge underground dam, one of the largest in the world; z) the limestone of the subsoil... A lot of people, especially since the community is not limited to a number of participants but can always integrate new members able to contribute to its functioning.

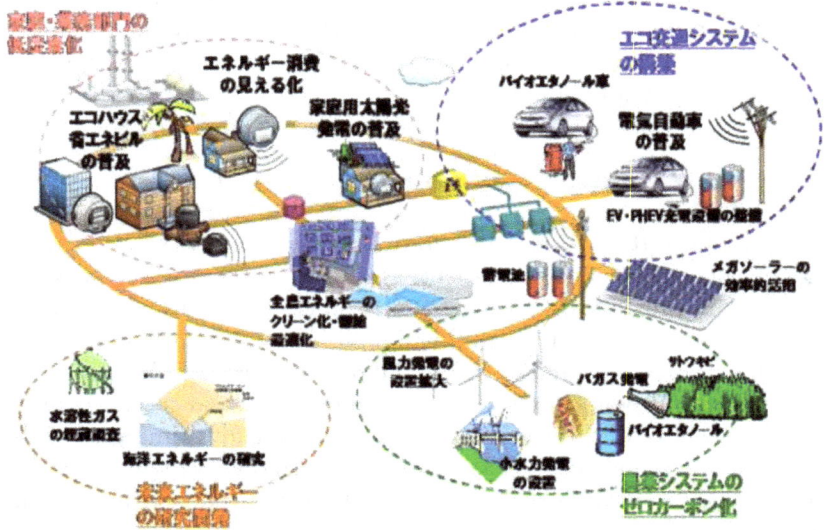

If the list remains open, the functioning is closed on itself. As shown in this schema published by the municipality of Miyako, the smart community is made up of chains of links, which are like so many small closed circuits. Whatever the schemas (and there are many of them), the smart community is always represented by finite loops of relationships; it is sometimes described as a "closed-loop society". Here we can visualise the systemic nature of this community: the smart community is not only a gathering of disparate elements, a mere aggregation of heterogeneous entities, but is first and foremost and fundamentally a *system*. This means that its members are caught up in interdependent and cooperative relationships, as in a body or in a machine, and that such collaborations between members are not subject to randomness, or to the wish of each one, but are fixed and determined beforehand. Each member, or rather should we say more accurately each *component*, fulfils functions assigned to it and must stick to them – otherwise it is the bug, the interruption, the malfunction. And this is the meaning of the word in computer science, where the loop designates a series of instructions that a program executes repeatedly.

This principle of relating does not therefore admit beings in their entirety, with their multiple characteristics, with the totality of their possibilities and modalities of being, but selects properties in them, the only ones judged useful for the functioning of the whole. Thus, the wind is slowed down in its movement and reduced to its ventilating capacity (in the eco-house for instance), or brought back to a source of energy (when it collaborates with the wind turbine); fish are agents controlling the quality of the water; the sun is also brought back to a capturable energy (in its collaboration with the photovoltaic panels); and so it is with all the components, including humans, who must likewise conform to the functions assigned to them and to the behaviour expected of them.

This ontological reduction is an essential feature of the smart community. Its very functioning is at stake. And this is where the "smartness" of this community is expressed, beyond the use of new technologies: everyone must collaborate *intelligently*, in other words in their place and function. Of course, information and communication technologies play an important role (and as such are represented in the centre of the schema by a wall of screens); they orchestrate the relations between the existing ones, through a set of measures, calculations of participation and efficiency, controls, notifications, and thus dictate behaviour, usage and good practice.

Miyako's smart community does not involve all the existing ones on the island, not because the community is still in the process of being developed and is for the moment a loose mesh, but because it only retains individuals useful for its functioning (individuals reduced to a function, as we have seen). Utility is a key concept here; each element has value only with regard to its usefulness in the system and is reduced to the useful role it plays within that system. This principle also establishes equality between components; none prevails, each has a role to play and must comply with it, each is in turn object or subject of decisions, user and used. Therefore the place of humans is radically redefined: in these chains of techno-social links, they are just one link among many others.

Enlarged view: Anthropocene and capitalism

The smart community of Miyako belongs to the physical space of Miyako: it is there, in the space of the island that the community deploys itself and with the elements that are present, either they were already there before (the dam, the mangrove, the sun, the fish, the humans...), or they have been specially brought in (the wind turbines, the photovoltaic panels, Toshiba's small electric car...). All the components are not local and consequently Miyako's smart community is linked to other places: places of design where architectures, assemblages, and functions are thought out, places of research and engineering. As the community also depends on places of governance, such as Tokyo, where objectives are defined, decisions are taken, and funding is granted; or beyond the nation, places such as the United Nations, from which emanate orientations, recommendations and agendas, such as the Sustainable Development Goals (SDGs) that Miyako follows. In this sense, the "local" of Miyako's smart community is also national, at times regional, at others international.

To fully understand what is happening in Miyako, we need to open up our focus, so to speak, in order to distinguish the overall movement in which Miyako's smart community participates and the background from which that community emerges. If we do that, we are faced with a global problem, that of an environmental situation that has become globally threatening to the life of many living species, including the human species; and an underlying problem of globalisation, that of a mode of production and consumption, that is, the problem of global capitalism.

There is first a kind of alarm, the formulation of an emergency that has taken the name of anthropocene. It is the sudden awareness that humans, through their activities, cause negative changes to the planet. These changes have a geological impact, which makes their impact irreversible.

While this statement of the destruction of the planet is not to be questioned, what can be questioned is the term anthropocene. Informed commentators, such as Bonneuil and Fressoz (2016), point out that to accuse Human, Anthropos, indiscriminately in this way is to deny the plural history of humanity and to deny the main causes of the destruction: causes relating to a specific way of life, linked to the worldwide expansion of the industrial capitalist system in the 19th century, the then colonial globalisation of Western empires, led by England, which not only formalised a mode of production and exchange on a global scale, but above all rationalised it through the exponential growth of the technique. This is therefore a rationalisation of production, consumption and transport, by means of technique.

All that is well known, and needs no further discussion here. I will take just one example borrowed from Feenberg (2010), of this technical rationalisation concerning Japan. During the modernisation of Japan that began in the Meiji period (1868–1912), the Mitsui family created in the 1910s the first Japanese department store, *Mitsukoshi*. Its floor was composed of tatami mats, a typically Japanese element in a building responding to a purchasing principle invented in the West. And as in the domestic space, customers had to take off their shoes. The success of the store quickly made the management of shoes and slippers that were substituted for them impossible. The technical mode of rationalisation of purchases in department stores could thus not tolerate the subsistence of a local element. Wooden floors therefore replaced the tatami mats after the 1923 earthquake that led to the entire rebuilding of Tokyo according to the idea of modernisation, from architectural arrangements to the wearing of Western clothing.

I cite this example simply to point out that the industrial mode of production led in the 19th century by the capitalist system and which developed throughout the 20th century on a global scale (in liberal or neoliberal democratic regimes as well as in socialist regimes or oligarchies or dictatorships), not only imposed technical rationalisation, but is also the cause of the present-day environmental situation, which should be more aptly called "capitalocene"[2].

Thus, it is in this context and genealogy that smart functioning emerges[3] and imposes itself as *the* solution to the environmental effects of capitalism. Like the phoenix rising from its ashes, a new world is taking shape on the ruins it has produced. But we must not be mistaken about the novelty of this world. If "smart" implies a rearrangement of the modes of relations between existing entities, if it imposes new forms of links, behaviours and uses, it does not in any way call into question the capitalist mode of production and consumption. On the contrary, it aims to maintain and preserve this dominant way of life and to be able to continue it in, or beside, increasingly ruined environments, as Anna Tsing points out.

---

[2]   The history of the "capitalocene" is analysed by Campagne (2017).

[3]   Another part of its genealogy is of course cybernetic thought; see in particular, Wiener (1989).

A new cosmology is thus taking shape, that of a *high-tech* global capitalism, made possible by the use of new technologies.

Close-up (2)

So, where are we in the smart community of Miyako? Certainly in one of the provinces of this "technological" capitalism. This province is not an independent one, but belongs to a larger whole, which I propose to call *the smart global community*.

This smart global community takes shape from the multiple sites that are developing smart arrangements around the world and from the many networks that link them, which are essential to their functioning. These include the movement of people: from administrators, engineers and designers, to the often-international workforce. In Miyako, Cuban officials and business leaders come to visit the mega-solar plant and to learn about energy experiments conducted on the island; collaborations are engaged with the State of Hawaii to increase the use of clean energy; the municipality of Miyako also teamed up with two other Japanese municipalities (Kityakyushu and Minamata) similarly engaged in building a smart community, in order to exchange information, knowledge, human resources and, together, "lead the creation of a low-carbon society in Japan, Asia, and even the world". Scientists come to conduct research. Working groups are set up and conferences are organised. Students in Global resource management, Life and Environmental Sciences, or Public Policy, come to Miyako for field trips. And special attention is given to the children, for getting into smart functioning also requires the education of future generations – this is where the mascot and her sidekick perform their role.

All the smart facilities that dot the island can be visited. The fields of solar panels and the wind turbines have been endowed with observatories; the eco-houses appear on tourist maps; the mangrove has been equipped with a wooden bridge to make it easier to cross by alleviating the inconvenience associated with bugs; and the underground dam even has its own museum. A small building called Eco-Park has also been built between sugarcane fields, in the car park of a refinery; it is the showroom of the smart in Miyako, that presents an overview of the project, by using panels, models and videos.

These are just a few examples of the network of relationships, specific to collaborations and the important promotional activity, which conditions the existence of the smart community of Miyako. This community also depends, like other smart configurations around the world, on capital flows, investors and companies involved in the development of smart projects, such as Toshiba, Cisco, Samsung, Acer, etc., all the major groups specialising in information technologies. And it is not just the flow of ideas, people and capital that links the various smart sites. Smart sites are also truly connected by the many underground and underwater cables required for digital networks (the Internet, data centres, everything that enables the circulation and processing of information) and energy distribution networks.

Miyako thus appears as *a* smart community (for the moment more imagined than completed) that is not isolated, and could not function in isolation, but is *a part* of a larger metabolism, in which each component is deeply dependent on the others to subsist as such.

Enlarged view: The unity of culture

These collaborations and connections between the smart sites thereby form a whole on a planetary scale, which makes a system. Hence, what I think is important to consider, and I would like to say a few words about this here, is the process of standardisation, on a global scale, that the smart brings about.

This process operates in a privileged way on the occasion of the many international events held periodically: forums, smart exhibitions, and smart summits such as the Smart City Expo World Congress, to mention but one. It also goes through the awarding of certifications on which the granting of funding notably depends, in other words selection, ranking and sometimes downgrading procedures. Miyako has thus been labelled an "Eco-Model city" by the Japanese government, but is not yet recognised as a "Future City", which is the higher label[4]. Standardisation also comes via the setting of objectives to be achieved (in terms of

---

[4]   See for instance the JPS (Japan For Sustainability) website. The aim of an "Eco-Model City" is to achieve a low-carbon society, whilst "Future City" initiatives (selected as the top-runner of Eco-Model Cities) concern in addition super-aging issues, dissemination worldwide, and green growth.

cutting carbon emission levels, for example), prescribing behaviours and uses, and developing norms and manufacturing standards, all of which are defined internationally (in other words, they apply to all, regardless of local anchorages).

One might think – and this is how they are presented – that these processes common to the world of the smart, which play on comparison, competition and competitiveness, promote inventiveness – or innovation, to use the language of this world. But what is at stake here is not to create, but to improve the global functioning. Possibilities may be exceeded, but only in continuity with what has been set. The technical functioning does not allow for deviation. In other words, the standardisation process is not just a consequence but also a principle that prevails in the smart: the smart functioning is a mode of conformation.

This mode of conformation seems to be able to take hold of all geographies. This contradicts the findings of Appadurai for whom "globalization is never a total project capturing all geographies with equal force" (2013: 67). The strength of technological functioning is indeed its universal character. If smart projects can be developed anywhere on the planet, if smart communities can be formed everywhere, it is because the technological functioning is not dependent on the local.

Of course, we can have culturally embedded conceptions or socially determined uses of technique. If we take the case of robots, for example, we could say very schematically that relations to them are rather dystopian in the West and rather empathetic in Asia, especially in Japan or Korea where laws for the rights of robots are promulgated. But the technique as a function is not determined by culture (in the anthropological sense). Technique obeys other laws (of physics, mathematics, computer science, etc.), which do not depend on sets of cultural meanings or social structures.

Technological functioning can therefore be applied everywhere independently of the specificities of local contexts; moreover, it is called upon to apply everywhere, in that it is also stated as a way of life. In the smart assemblages of existing entities, the universalism of technical reason appears as a cultural principle. This leads me to say that the smart global community expresses a kind of *perspectivism*, distributing components of different natures but obeying the same culture. But unlike the Amerindian perspectivism highlighted by Viveiros de Castro[5], the common

---

[5]   In his remarkable study of Amerindian perspectivism, which also constitutes an important reflection on the meaning of "nature" and "culture", Viveiros de Castro

culture here is not anthropological, but technological (and even more, algorithmic).

Consequently, the debates and concrete negotiations provoked by globalisation, between a universalism of techno-capitalist reason and the diversity of cultural formations (Appadurai 2005, Bhabha 2007), no longer arise in the case of the smart. Questions of appropriation disappear; there may be debates on uses, on exclusions (because not everybody is part of it), but the functioning as such is not debated.

Where previously one or two centres unilaterally disseminated their way of being to the whole world, different ways of being are now proposing to take charge of the production of the same global functioning. Or to put it differently, each local, in spite of its differences, produces one and the same global.

The smart global community thus appears to be multi-sited: not, to respect the misused concept of Marcus (1995), because it is deployed on several sites, but because it is made up of parts linked by the same instance. These multiple parts of a globalised common whole can be seen as so many "worlding nodes", to use the beautiful expression coined by Roy and Ong (2011) about the new Asian urbanism[6]; nodes that in the case of the smart participate in the same planetary becoming commanded by the same principle of technological universalism.

Close-up (3)

The smart community of Miyako can therefore be seen as *a part*, both sited and in itself global. But then, we still have to account for something that seems to oppose this, when one listens to and observes the way the Miyako's smart community describes itself, which, on the contrary,

---

suggests "the expression 'multinaturalism', to designate one of the contrastive features of Amerindian thought in relation to Western 'multiculturalist' cosmologies. Where the latter are founded on the mutual implication of the unity of nature and the plurality of cultures – the first guaranteed by the objective universality of body and substance, the second generated by the subjective particularity of spirit and meaning – the Amerindian conception would suppose a spiritual unity and a corporeal diversity. Here, culture or the subject would be the form of the universal, whilst nature or the object would be the form of the particular." (1998: 470).

[6] Worlding nodes can be seen "as a particular nexus of situated and transnational ideas, institutions, actors, and practices that may be variously drawn together for solving particular problems" (p. 4). See also Collier, S.J., Ong A. (2005).

never stops highlighting its specificities. Like the defence of a certain art of living, combining authenticity, simplicity and quietness, far from the frantic rhythms of the big cities. Or the beauty of the landscape and nature. Or again the recognition of the wisdom of the elders and the perpetuation of ancient practices that suddenly become smart, such as collecting ground water by means of an underground dam, which takes up a very old practice on the island of building wells and underground tunnels in which one would go down to get water; or the method of purifying water using algae and micro-organisms – something which, in the words of the municipality, "seems to be a primitive low technology but [...] is a wise use of natural phenomena, [...] a real smart technology for our life" (Miyako-jima City Water Authority 2014: 4).

Does this mean that even if we are witnessing the fabrication of an a-cultural global, for all that, "culture" would nevertheless not totally disappear?

While it is still too early to answer this question, we can nevertheless examine three possible, non-exclusive possibilities. First, local specificities may remain for a while, but will eventually disappear, like the tatami mats in the Mitsukoshi department store. If they all disappear, then in Miyako only a localised global with no local will remain. The precursor case that immediately comes to mind is the international smart city of Songdo (South Korea), built as a turnkey model that can be transposable anywhere else in the world.

Second, specificities of Miyako, reduced to the rank of acceptable differences, which are not useful for the functioning but do not hinder it either, will continue to exist in ignorance or indifference. It is those, with no value and no importance, which will escape the system.

Third, specificities are called to be maintained as specificities, or more precisely as *particularisms*. These are differences, specific to each sited community, which have a role to play in the global assemblage[7]. They

---

[7]   It can be seen as a re-actualisation of the utilitarianism of John Stuart Mill, in which use would replace production: "These [outlying possessions of ours] are hardly to be looked upon as countries... but more properly as outlying agricultural or manufacturing estates belonging to a larger community. Our West Indian colonies, for example, cannot be regarded as countries with a productive capital of their own... [but are rather] the place where England finds it convenient to carry on the production of sugar, coffee and a few other tropical commodities", quoted by Said (1993: 59).

are therefore caught up in the common functional regime (with what this implies, as we have seen, of assignment, dependence and ontological reduction). They may need to be recontextualised – assembling often implies a recontextualisation of the elements that are assembled (or, to put it another way, a re-reading of the local). In sum, they can be seen as the expression of a *style*: a variation from the inside, a way of differentiating oneself within the same space of reference and functioning.

The particularisms of Miyako would probably refer to the economy of leisure. Preserving in the smart global community the possibility of leisure could indeed be the *function* of the Miyako smart community and the stake, or utility, of its participation. The "art of being global", to use the expression coined by Roy and Ong (2011), is perhaps also that: to exist in the world to come by finding the way to play in it a role *as a full part*.

Conclusion

The systemic character demanded by the current technologies at the core of the smart seems to be producing something new: the radicality with which ways of life are being univocally captured. We could say that life is thus taken by a new ultra-powerful and de facto unifying apparatus; an apparatus in the sense of which Agamben has defined it (2009), that is to say a system that captures substance for its transformation into a subject; and the smart apparatus subjugates not only human life, but all the substances that are useful. A world defined by the technological condition is thus taking shape. Japan is already projecting itself into a *super smart* society, the so-called "society 5.0", in which cyberspace (or virtual space) and physical space (or real space) are linked by the Internet of Things and the use of artificial intelligence optimises everything useful, and intends to propose it as a guiding principle from Japan to the world.

References

Agamben Giorgio, *What Is an Apparatus? and Other Essays*, Stanford, Stanford University Press, 2009.

Appadurai Arjun, *Modernity at Large. Cultural Dimensions of Globalization*, Minneapolis, University of Minnesota Press, 1996.

Appadurai Arjun, *The Future as Cultural Fact: Essays on the Global Condition*, London, Verso, 2013.

Bhabha Homi K., *The Location of Culture*, New York, Routledge, 1994.

Bonneuil Christophe, Fressoz Jean-Baptiste, *The Shock of the Anthropocene: The Earth, History and Us*, London, Verso, 2016.

Campagne Armel, *Le capitalocène. Aux racines historiques du dérèglement climatique*, Paris, Éditions Divergences, 2017.

Collier S.J., Ong A. (eds.), *Global Assemblages: Technology, Politics, and Ethics as Anthropological Problems*, Malden, Blackwell, 2005.

Feenberg Andrew, *Between Reason and Experience*, Cambridge, Massachusetts Institute of Technology Press, 2010.

Marcus George E., "Ethnography in/of the World System: The Emergence of Multi-Sited Ethnography", in *Annual Review of Anthropology*, vol. 24, 1995, p. 95–117.

Miyakojima City, *Declaration of Eco Island*, Okinawa, May 31th 2008.

Miyako-jima City Water Authority (ed.), *Welcome to Sodeyama Treatment Plant*, 2014.

Roy Ananya, Ong Aihwa, *Worlding Cities. Asian Experiments and the Art of Being Global*, Malden, Wiley-Blackwell, 2011.

Said Edward W., *Culture and Imperialism*, New York, First Vintage Books Edition, 1993.

Toshiba Review, *Science and Technology Highlights*, 2015.

Tsing Anna L., *The Mushroom at the End of the World: On the Possibility of Life in Capitalist Ruins*, Princeton, Princeton University Press, 2015.

Viveiros de Castro Eduardo, "Cosmological Deixis and Amerindian Perspectivism", in *The Journal of the Royal Anthropological Institute*, vol. 4, no. 3, 1998, p. 469–488.

Wiener Norbert, *The Human Use of Human Beings. Cybernetics and Society* [1950], London, Free Association Books, 1989.

What happened to community? How Latour's actor-network theory deals with this key notion in sociology

RÉMI ASTRUC

Translated by Tara Ostiguy

Introduction

The re-description of the world which is at the heart of Bruno Latour's ambitious scientific project carried out over the last thirty years (a project that will mainly be discussed here through the readings of three of his works: *Down to Earth*, 2019; *An Inquiry Into Modes of Existence*, 2012; and, especially, *Reassembling the Social – An Introduction to the Actor-Network Theory*, 2005), which entails nothing less than a renewal of sociology itself, radially overlooks the notion/concept/idea and even the very word "community". For those who, like us, place this notion at the heart of their vision of the world (and of the most essential political struggles; see Astruc 2016)[1], the ability to know how to justify its main-tenance and defend its "scientific" pertinence becomes what is truly at stake. This is particularly true at a moment where this sociological theory and its herald enjoy – for good reasons it would seem to us moreover – an undivided and, at present, almost hegemonic attention in France[2].

---

[1]   The capital C in "Community" will indicate the concept we are seeking to defend in this text. That is, the power of the idea of the common, a universal aspiration that would animate humankind. It distinguishes itself from "community", with a lower case c, that will designate actual and effective groupings of individuals that are often identity-based. For further developments on this matter, see chapter 1 of our essay *Nous?* (Astruc 2016).

[2]   He would appear to be the most cited French thinker abroad (cf. introduction of Latour by Adèle Van Reth during his appearance on radio France Culture for the series "Profession philosophe"). He is the recipient of the prestigious Holberg prize

In our view, this interest is explained in particular by the new weight of ecological and environmental crisis in our lives (Latour 2015). It reveals, more bluntly than ever before, the crisis of occidental modernity, long denounced by the author (Latour 1991). His proposals for a different understanding of our society and, as a consequence, revising the sociology that studies it, in order to redetermine "how to act collectively", thus rings not only "just" but falls in a way at a timely moment – as a last recourse, in the hopes of finally knowing "how to orient ourselves politically" (the subtitle to the French-language edition of *Down to Earth*) before it is perhaps too late.

The degree of focus that Latour gives to the terrestrial environment, to non-humans, as well as to beings that are "living or almost" – such as the planet, viruses, rivers or gods – would appear to invite us to construct a *thought of Community* (at the very least a community "of destiny": Man/Earth, Human/Non-human, etc.). Nonetheless, his sociology, if it is concerned with the "common", paradoxically unfolds without any recourse to the notion of "Community". Let us be clear that the essential issue for us does not lie in a quarrel over the terms of a debate. That is to say, the debate surrounding Latour's potentially understandable rejection of a concept "loaded" with the weight of two-hundred years of sociology in which he invites us to break with. Nor is our fundamental issue the substance of the debate or its position, as expressed by the author, according to which Community would be but an illusion of the sociologist (or philosopher): it is after all logical, in light of the premises of ANT and of *An Inquiry Into Modes of Existence*, which claims to situate itself within a strict "plane of immanence" and to construct a "flat ontology" (Vibert 2016). We will come back to this later. The principal issue for us will be to contest the fact that the sociology of the actor-network, in placing itself within a strictly individual framework at the level of the actors – and refusing in particular all symbolic origins of the social (Maniglier 2007), has driven out all "*communal affect*" from its description as from its comprehension of human formations. What it implies is that this approach refutes the existence of a "tropism", of a "power" or of an "anthropological instinct" that could alone, in our view, particularly within this indecisive era, orient us towards this alliance that is necessary

---

in 2013 and the object of sustained media attention in France for some years. The Ministry of Ecology has financially supported the implementation of some of his actions.

both for our survival and the survival of our environment in general. For what could encourage us – notably to act – in this case, apart from the single frontal collision with a wall encountered at the bottom of the dead-end itself? And obviously no one wishes to entrust their recovery/destiny to a wall…

Hence the proposition we would like to explore here: can we not add up their respective strengths and reconcile, in part, these two conceptions of the social – the sociology of the actor-network and the philosophical thought on Community – that seem, in appearance, antagonistic to one another[3]? With a view to enriching the real understanding of the "social in the making", as promised by ANT, is it not then possible to cross the Latourian description of what exists – which claims to be "realistic" and to refer only to what is: attachments forming a network – with an understanding of these attachments that would be neither idealist or "ideological" (belonging to the realm of belief) but rather *differentialist*? Could such an understanding, which could thus welcome varying *degrees* of intensity of these attachments, in addition to the different planes (religious, technical, scientific, etc.) on which they are deployed, therefore make a useful purpose of the concept of Community? It will be possible, as we will see, and not by a radical redefinition of this concept but, rather, by a refined understanding of it.

In order to do this, it is necessary to first go back to the main principles on which this sociology is founded and, most importantly, to the "objective" research protocol that makes up its strength. Secondly, it will be necessary to determine what place is left in a model with such "realistic" claims for a thought of Community that is not only a pure imaginary construct deriving from mere belief. Finally, we shall see that it is in redefining the modes of appearance of Community that we likely define it best. Moreover, we will see that the conception of the social as "fluid", put forward by Latour himself, is revealed to be of particular use in going beyond the measures his sociology employs to prevent the notion of Community.

---

[3] We would like to speak here, in particular, about the rich and diverse thought of the Community elaborated by thinkers such as Georges Bataille, Maurice Blanchot, Jean-Luc Nancy, Giorgio Agamben and Roberto Esposito to cite only the most important philosophers concerned.

The main principles of this sociology and the reasons for the exclusion of community: What alone exists, according to ANT

In order to grasp its specificity, let us begin by recalling that this approach finds its point of departure in the sociology *of sciences*; it is, above all, the description of the latter as a "network" (and thus scientific objectivity as a product of this network) that acts as a framework to this radically empiricist sociology. The only reality it detects is therefore the construction of chains of multiple actors. A celebrated event as, for example, "Pastor's discovery of penicillin" is reread in this optic no longer as a discovery brought to fruition by the individual genius of a great man and his exposing of a hidden phenomenon of biology. Rather, it is seen as a strict establishment of a network that is constituted by the cooperation of a man, Pasteur, along with a long list of "actors", that participate to a certain degree on the same level as that of the discovery itself. The participating actors in the matter at hand include microbes, test tubes, a laboratory, financiers (of this laboratory), lab benches, scientific reports, etc. (Latour 1985).

It is this radically empiricist concept of scientific "reality" (of what science is "really" made of: in truth of all of these actors, says Latour) that was later extended to the description of other fields beyond science (law, politics, art, religion, etc.) and then to the description of the "social" as a whole. Within this model, everything that exists then would thus come *in fine* from *networks* that unfold on different planes of existence (legal, political, scientific, etc.: see *An Inquiry into Modes of Existence* that lists at least twelve), each having its irreducible "mode of truth" and institutions that legitimise them. All the while, these same institutions often make the materiality of these networks disappear before our very eyes by "naturalising" them; that is to say, by making them appear as always already there and always already formed.

This is why, for Bruno Latour, there is no "society" – in the sense that man would not *always already* live "in society" – there is no social life that pre-exists networks and no "social" foundation on which this would be deployed. There are only actors that perpetually seek to construct their networks in order to maintain themselves: namely, *ad hoc* "associations" that are more or less durable, more or less solid and more or less efficient. And if there is no "society", there can therefore neither be "community", according to the classical Tönnesian notion of the

Gemeinschaft-Gesellschaft couple (Tönnies 2010). That is, there is in reality no superior or transcendental force presiding over the grouping of humans, and so no *social instinct* that would drive humankind to gather and form "societies", but rather only a reality that drives them to associate in an opportunistic manner. Thus, no "social force", no social relations, no "social question", or social context, etc., that would permit us to explain our behaviour and orient our actions within a sociology that claims to be *truly* "realistic". In summary, the "social", according to this sociology, does not exist as such – it is always made of something else, "of other matter" (possibly "of" the religious, "of" the technical, "of" the political, etc.). That is, different specific but interconnected spheres of human action, different "modes of existence" of realities, beings or things.

Indeed, if there is no Society according to this sociology (as we understand it, namely, no platonic idea of society), it nonetheless recognises, without difficulty whatsoever, the existence of human groupings that are in turn always meant to be real and specific: the société *française*, the so called "société anonyme" (SA) X or Y (a particular company), the Société des gens de Lettres (SGDL), just as there was the société d'Ancien Régime, or the Société des Nations (SDN). Of course, on the basis of this same model, this sociology would without a doubt be ready to admit that there exists not *a* Community but communit*ies*. This is to say, particular forms of human associations: the community of AIDS patients[4], the North African community in France, the village community of Trifouillis-les-Oies, the EEC (at least before its transition to the European "Union"), etc.

The problem for "us" (that is, the whole of the philosophy on Community, following Bataille, Blanchot, Nancy, or Agamben and Esposito, as well as just about the rest of sociology)[5], could thus be stated in these terms: if it is not "Community" – as acting force of the collective-being, power of being "in-common" or *clinamen* of existence understood as "compearance" (Nancy 1991), that is to say, *always already* social – what could it be that drives us to gather together and is capable of producing

---

[4]   As it is referenced in footnote 3 of page 35 in *Reassembling the Social.* This is one of the rare occurrences of this word in the book…

[5]   Specifically in the wake of Louis Dumont's anthropology or of MAUSS (antiutilitarian movement in the social sciences) or even of Cornélius Castoriadis of *The Imaginary Institute of Society.* Cf. Vibert 2006.

the desire or need for such a meeting[6]? Latour's sociology, because it purports to be interested only in what "really" exists and "is visible", remains largely silent on the sources or causes of what produces these networks which he undertakes to describe.

For our part, we defend the idea that it is this very *lack*, the absence of the manifestation of Community (subsequently understood as a kind of "*deus absconditus*"), that produces the need for Community in humankind. If we maintain a belief in the existence of such a force that is hidden but active, it is that we think that it is this very lack that produces the desire for its advent and thereby directs humankind and makes it act *in reality*. For if it is not a centripetal force that incites humans to join together in order to fully realise their humanity (linked to the perception of an "existential need", a need for a fuller and richer life that would be fulfilled by Community) how can we continue to believe that we could possibly orient ourselves – let alone save ourselves – in the midst of the ecological crisis we currently face?

The new prominence given to Latour in France – it is to be noted he has long had a considerable influence in the Anglo-Saxon world – is, as we have noted, connected to the difficulties in which we now find ourselves in the use of *old modes of thought* to comprehend what is at present happening to us. There exists an impossibility of accounting for certain realities according to these modes of thought. This has forced us to rethink anew the ecological crisis and everything it entails: the collapse of life and the impossibility of sharing wealth and space (the fact, as Latour clearly explains in *Down to Earth*, that we live and consume as if we possessed two and a half planets). In addition to this, there is the issue of a broader crisis of our Western model of civilisation (in Latour's terms of "modernity" as a whole); all of these factors together have contributed to increasing the pertinence of this radically alternative sociological model.

This model depends on an initial methodological requirement that aims to rectify the so-called "errors" of other models, which is also – in fact – the road envisioned to avoid our present day obstacles: to carry out a systematic and enriched *re-description* of the social (that is, of the modes of social assemblage). This description notably includes

---

[6]   Unless one were to think, in a Hobbesian perspective, that this meeting is always negative; that is to say, constrained by adversity.

the integration of the multitude of beings that surround us – human, non-human, objects but also "Gaïa" (the "Earth-system") – which are usually excluded from traditional sociological thought. The overall ambition, thanks to this *more "realistic" montage* of the real, is to arrive at "altering the path of society" by giving us the means to act upon it (Latour 2005: 9).

It is thus what actor-network sociology has strived to do since the 1980s by way of the successive re-description of the experimental conditions of science, law, religion, art, politics, etc., to which Latour has devoted himself in his various works. That is to say, not attack, weaken, or destroy the certainties and foundations of these fields but, rather, reconstruct them with more solidity, in a more coherent way, to be able then to articulate their claims in the coming negotiations vis-a-vis our way of life. To this end was principally the effort of eliminating the "chimeras" of the "social" to thus restore its efficacy, according to the author, to *politics*.

What has currently made this model so influential is that its initial premise, one which not only seemed bold but even risky only a decade ago, seems now and, increasingly more, commonplace: there is *visibly no "society"*, states the actor-network theory, in the sense of an all constituted and already present entity that could explain our situation and our behaviour[7]. Of course, this observation should not be confounded with the ideological position that Margaret Thatcher subscribed to when she infamously declared in 1987 "there is no such thing as society". This affirmation ultimately derived from her neo-liberal creed and a broadly *utilitarian* vision of the social bond. Here, it is rather an observation on the nature of society that intends to be "neutral" and "realistic", which could be articulated as follows: *we do not come together without reason*. And if we gather *all the same*, it is not because we want to "make society", or that we are driven by a mysterious force to "make community".

Thus, the novelty here is that the idea of "society" now is no longer undermined by an ideological positioning but rather by a somewhat careful observation of the realities of the contemporary social world. We would have passed, so to speak, from an "ideological" moment,

---

[7]　"For a long time I believed I lived in society..." wrote François Dubet, even if it was *in fine* to insist on the importance of this notion (Dubet 2009).

constituted by opposing theses concerning the interpretation of a reality that is still obscure, to a "descriptive" moment – that of a reality that has become clearer. It is for this reason that this analysis claims "objectivity" and is to some extent widely shared in the political spectrum today, as much by the neoconservatives of the right as by proponents of the revolutionary "ultra-left". It is the reason why the description in the citation that follows – of the "social carcass" which "never ceases to decompose and recompose", to let now perceive the reticular character of the social – does not come, as we might think, from Latour himself or from a sociologist of the actor-network theory but from the contemporary proponents of revolutionary communism:

> No society, then, but worlds […] There is no social sky above our heads, there is only us and the ensemble of ties, friendships, enmities, and the actual proximities and distances that we experience. There are only sets of us, eminently situated powers, and their capacity to extend their ramifications to the very heart of the social carcass that never ceases to decompose and recompose. A swarming of worlds, a world made of a heap of worlds and thus traversed by conflict between them, attractions and repulsions. (Comité invisible 2014: 195–196)

As surprising as this may seem, it should be noted that at present we are increasingly witness to the proclamation of "the death of society" (at least in the Western world), on which there are certain agreed upon yet fiercely opposed political sensibilities. Such a consensus seems to lend credibility to the original intuition of the actor-network theory: the illusion of the social, once dissipated, will reveal that which veritably "ties us": namely, ties that are fragile, shifting (individually revocable) and always in need of confirmation and mending. That is, networks of bonds that are held together by nothing beyond their own strength. No substrate or hypostasis that would constitute "Society" and keep the whole together but, rather, a multitude of connections in the making, a myriad of social processes, *associations* (such is the term employed by Latour) or, to be even more precise, *processes of association.*

The classical view of "Society" as always-already-all-constituted had the effect of masking and even preventing further developments, its force residing precisely in its resistance to redeployment: "Society" would have been, in reality, ultimately only the very political name for a social inertia or entropy. Its disappearance would correspond then to the liberation of a power, the possibility to finally be able to conceive of the reorganisation of the social. However, the question remains: how and by virtue of what[8]?

The common view on this matter evidently leads to radically opposing conclusions: for the Invisible Committee, which is cited above, this liberation of the molecular force of social organisation should permit... the construction of the "Community". Indeed, the disappearance of Society is, to some extent, the good news that allows the reappearance of the former. It even kindles hope of its imminent advent *by way of* Revolution. The Community then would not vanish into the movement that makes "pseudo" Society disappear but, on the contrary, would be revealed by this very movement as what orients (or should orient) the bonds now free to recompose. This signifies that, for the Invisible Committee, if society does not exists – or no longer exists – the "Community" does indeed exist and, in a sense, more so than ever before. It is even the only thing that counts at present: the disappearance of society has indeed liberated a horizon that would be constituted by the only desirable, "liveable", form of association... what, evidently, the Latourian description of the social cannot in this way conceive[9].

Should we continue to make room for the notion of community?

Of course, Latour's position on the matter is quite different. Logically, from an ANT perspective, if there is no Society – as we have already noted – there can therefore neither be Community; it is another form of the same sociological "mirage". This, in passing, incidentally resolves the quarrel over the historicity of forms and closes the debate on

---

[8]   One critique of this sociology, which we will not expound on here, is precisely that it seems to open the way to a liberation that is not problematised. The critique follows that, ultimately, it seems to liberate nothing more than a pure liberty of the actors, revealing an ideological proximity (under the guise of escaping such ideologies) to economic liberalism.

[9]   Here it would seem that we touch upon an aporia of Latour's system: the evacuation of politics (as ideological struggle that has little concern for truth) in favour of a strict "scientific" description of the real must, nonetheless, lead back to this very same politics at the end of the process. Politics would reappear as the capacity to act on the real, resulting from negotiations between actors according to the values they hold (hence, their ideologies) – as such, it cannot be an entirely convincing claim.

the supposed anteriority of Community or Society. The notion of "Community", according to Latour, would thus fall within this "sociology of the social", which replaces with concepts that are both erudite and exogenous – mysterious forces that are at once invisible and unverifiable – the *experience* that the actors *really* live without any need for complicated abstractions. To guard oneself against such "illusions", the tenet and operative word of his sociology is thus to always and only "follow the actors themselves" and their "*real*" experiences. Therefore, the research protocol reveals itself to be very concrete: in order to follow associations and learn to identify them, it is enough to learn to recognise the "traces" which they cannot help but leave behind.

In *Reassembling the Social*, Latour explains that if something exists it will, as a matter of fact, leave clues of its existence that researchers should be able to detect. If it is otherwise, it becomes entirely impossible to affirm with any certainty that this thing exists and we could, at any rate, never be able to say anything whatsoever about it. The only real, realistic or objective criteria to attest to the existence of a "social group", indeed even a given "society" or a "community", are therefore the following: to focus on *visibility*, which in turn reveals the attachments (the "translations" that interlocking actors require), the *knots* that form in the network (Latour 2005: 46). This is the price to be paid for a truly realistic sociology, says Latour.

Hence the recommendation given to ANT sociologists in search of associations to uncover: to start from the "controversies", notably scientific, of "disputed facts" (forms of conflictuality) that are patent signs that the network exists. That is to say, evidence that it strives to maintain itself or expand. It is what the author of *Reassembling the Social* calls the "cost" of attachments, about which he develops several criteria for identification. A group becomes visible –and thus exists –when:

- it acquires a leader or spokesperson, denominated as "group-maker" or "responsible for cohesion" ("No flock of sheep without a shepherd"), summarises Latour (*ibid.*: 48);
- that its cohesion is founded on the exclusion of other groups;
- that it strives to distinguish itself from these other groups by working towards reinforcing its own borders;
- it mobilises professionals to assert its existence: namely sociologists, or journalists, but also acquires and makes use of statistics, in short, of the social sciences itself. The identification of a group by

researchers that study it, directly participates as such in the establishment of this very group's existence.

- Finally, when it attemptsto acquire a definition and forms, for example, by displaying principles or by exhibiting representations (symbols, totems, etc.).

If we keep in mind what is of particular interest to us here, namely the question of Community, we see that these so-called "objective" criteria contribute, in the name of realism, to a radical simplification of what could be understood as a group. As a matter of fact, they delineate nothing more than a very particular and limited version of what we could consider to be "community".

This empirical understanding of reality, notably based on "social conflictuality", intended to protect from the illusions of theory, can in fact only highlight communit*ies* (with a lower case c) that are singular and particularising. Such communit*ies* diverge from, and even betray, the Community (upper case c) as a generic ideal that is not particularised and not particularising. Indeed, the criteria maintained here strongly filters our grasp of what is considered to be uniquely real and, thus, can only ever reveal the first community as existing and not the second. We could therefore oppose this sociology and argue that it is not because types of social assemblages exist that they appear to researchers of the actor-network theory but, on the contrary, that the criteria that is held is what makes them appear in the first place. That is to say, they appear by virtue of a manifest logical bias.

Conversely, a wider conception of the nature of Community eludes this criteria and renders it inadequate: the question of leaders is indeed largely in contradiction with the Community as an ideal of relations that are *a priori* horizontal and relatively egalitarian. The exclusion of other groups is in contradiction with the communal momentum itself, based on a group hospitality that is *a priori* maximal; moreover, the reinforcement of borders appears to be in contradiction with a disposition that is inclusive, *a priori* without boundaries that characterise the desire for Community. The recourse to professionals that study it, escapes temporality and, in particular, the epiphanic dimension of the "event" that the Community seeks to be. Finally, if the Community indeed acquires sensitive and aesthetic forms, as we will see below (it positions itself, in particular, within a narrative framework), the identity content of these forms is less important than the act of *telling itself* – that is, performance and sharing more than conflict (Astruc 2016: chapter "Pourquoi le récit?").

We see these objections to the sociological conception of the actor-network theory consistently returning to the matter of the "a priori" formulation. Indeed, a group is effectively never "a priori" what it is in reality; however, this *a priori* is indeed nonetheless what is going to shape, despite all real distortions incurred immediately afterwards, the various forms that the project of association will take in reality. Therefore, it is a factor that should be taken into consideration in understanding this reality. More generally, does "following what is real" necessarily mean that only that which appears to us as real exists? *An Inquiry into Modes of Existence*, released in 2012, fortunately renders this matter more complex by taking into account further varied "modes of existence" and, thus, different modes of visibility or apparitions according to the beings in question. This permitted the introduction of several realities into the category of what exists that initially eluded the actor-network theory's grasp in its original formulation.

In fact, if something does not appear on the ANT sociologist's radar, it does not mean that such a thing does not exist but, rather, simply that he does not see it: he does not *know* how to see it as he is ill equipped. This is naturally of great importance for us, for whom the "Community" is always *in potential* and thus invisible, but who maintain that it nevertheless indeed exists – *all the more so* by the fact that it does not manifest in reality in the form of a constituted group[10]. For it nonetheless works towards closer relations amongst humankind and produces associations that are the fruit of its influence. Defined as such, the Community is a force that exists *in its effects*, for it does indeed provoke action, it produces forms of human associations. The latter are precisely the traces it leaves behind in reality.

Ultimately, ANT's sociology would therefore appear to be like a *filter* that permits the fine observation of reality and the discernment, in particular, of the granularity of associations. However:

---

[10]   What is visible is indeed the effect (the groups) and not the Community that precedes it, which is not otherwise visible by itself; it is "community(ies) in potential" cf. Astruc 2016, beginning of chapter 2. In keeping with Agamben (1990), we could say that the absence-of-being of the Community is the empty space of identity and it is its revolutionary power.

1. It does not allow to discriminate, in an "a priori" manner at any rate, between different *forms* of associations. It demonstrates a particular incapacity to take into account differences in "quality of assemblage" (it does not allow to discriminate among that which would arise, for example, from differences between the mode of association of "society" and the mode of association of "community"); Moreover, it is quite uncertain whether it is better able to do so *a posteriori*, once the associations have been made.

2. For it does not allow to distinguish the differential *force* of these attachments. ANT perceives "society", like "community", as "connectors", among others, that are valued by their "success", which is measured according to the number of associations – the size of the network – and duration – the longevity of the network – as the only visible criteria for description.

In a model that views Community as a *disposition of being*, or an anthropological, even cosmological, *vocation* – that is to say, as a consequence of our existence within the "network" of the living and even that of the "Earth-system" – Community inevitably falls under the ANT radar. It is naturally invisible or, in the least, it does not appear under the mode of appearance established by this sociology; yet it nonetheless exists, albeit in a different manner.

How does it exist then? Obviously, less according to criteria that are quantitative and "real" than to those that are qualitative and, say, relative. Thus, what remains inconceivable within the actor-network model is that the Community draws its strength *by its own failure* (and notably its failure to appear, to be actualised in reality). It is thus all the more efficient and active as unrealisable and precisely *because* it is unrealisable (it acts by virtue of its *lack*, as we have noted above). It is in the end a desirable horizon, one that orients and frames collective action. Upon close inspection, it is a VALUE and, as a value, shapes the actions of men. More than a simple "connector" – according to the ANT terminology forwarded in *Reassembling the Social*[11] – that would be real and actualised, the Community would instead correspond to an "attractor", specified in the revised model of *Down to Earth*. In other words, it would be the orientation of affect.

---

[11] If Latour is a "relativist", as his detractors accuse him of being, it is above all because his sociology is unable to "a priori" discriminate between values…

However, if there is indeed something essential that the actor-network theory teaches us, it is the necessity – if we wish to maintain the pertinence of the concept of Community (as active entity and descriptive category) – to see the Community *as a process* and not a given. This is contrary to what the term, which is loaded with ambiguity on the matter, evokes: it could seem to designate an entity that is already there. Therefore, if there is one point upon which we can fully agree with ANT, it is precisely on this labile characteristic: always fluctuating, always having to reinforce or affirm associations and, most importantly, the Community (in the making) itself. Perhaps it would be best then to replace this term with "communitising" or "communitization" (as employed by Max Weber 2019) to be clearer? It might well be the case.

There remains one point to which we should return before being able to conclude this thought: *in spite of all of this*, how do we account for the existence of the Community without compromising the empiricist rigour that constitutes ANT's strength? That is the decisive question to be able to affirm that our approach is just as "realistic" or scientific as that of Latour's[12]. In other words, it is a matter of showing how the Community, despite its nature of "attractor" and its invisibility, can nonetheless incontestably appear.

How can the community appear?

As the aforementioned quote from the Invisible Committee suggests, it is against a backdrop of battle – a struggle between worlds – that the Community can make its influence felt. It is inseparable from a certain natural violence of attachments (friendships and enmities are woven together and clash with one another), at least it emerges out of conflict and controversy[13]. Community then indeed appears, according to the logic of ANT, and we can even argue that it "territorialises" itself, in a way, within the panorama as a desirable horizon[14]. Therefore, we can

---

[12] Taking the risk of positioning ourselves within this field is the only way to dialogue/negotiate with Latour and ANT – that is, in speaking the same language and in advocating, as they do, for what is "real". Otherwise, how can one hope to be taken seriously? Controversy should be made possible; on this point, they are correct.

[13] In this regard (that of scientific controversy), Community would enter into ANT's modes of visibility (and thus existence) of "realities". However, we naturally cannot content ourselves with this.

[14] Not necessarily resolution but acceptance and going beyond social conflictuality.

consequently strive to say something about it. We can, in fact, begin to follow it like Latour's theory invites us to do for any given "actor-network". The Community expresses itself (translates itself) through the "oeuvres" that are its trace. Just as in Reassembling Society, we can attempt to make a typology to identify the different types of traces (surely quite different from those of ANT) that seem to be able to affirm its existence.

1. The Community manifests itself in the first place through *aesthetic expressions*; it is perhaps here where the Community appears most clearly today. Works of art testify to the human aspiration for Community in both their specificity and general vocation. All "writing-literature", as Jean-Luc Nancy terms it, cannot but be precisely the trace of this Community. All art forms, perhaps most of all literature, testify in their own right to its existence, it is a "telling" of the Community. We have thus shown elsewhere (Astruc 2016) how the Community tells *itself* through the solo of a dancer, a novel by Genêt, a story by Kafka, the poetry arising out of a student strike, the mythological accounts of a Melanesian tribe, and post-exotic literature amongst other innumerable examples. Here, the Community tells *itself*; that is to say, it is in this way that it expresses itself and unveils itself to humankind[15].

2. However, we also find traces of the Community in certain *lived experiences*, instances of which are equally innumerable: intense life experiences that are born from sudden human relations and perceived as a form of absolute plenitude. Let us call such happenings "ecstatic experiences". Indeed, what is remarkable about the Community is that, when man does experience it in certain specific circumstances, the latter impresses upon them an overwhelming desire to rediscover this state of communion with others (composed of friendship, brotherhood, sharing and joy). Over the course of a Revolution, a riot, a strike, a demonstration, a party, a concert, an occupation, or even an embrace, the memory of lived relations – fragile yet strong – most lastingly and deeply imprint

---

[15]   Although extremely diverse, the Community is nevertheless very determined but as "whatever" ("defined but uniquely within the empty space of the example" says Agamben, 1990). For other examples, see the dissertation of Julie Brugier "Marginalité et communauté dans les œuvres de W. Faulkner, R. de Queiroz et M. Condé", or J.-L. Nancy's thought in *La Comparution* for a more philosophical perspective.

themselves in the being of those individuals who experienced them. So deeply are they entrenched, that they often become the yardstick by which all other relations are measured, compelling these individuals to recover the plenitude of life they have only been able to glimpse. It is in this way that "communisation" is nothing more than the epiphanic memory of relations that are far stronger and richer than the mere association: ties that radically transform the nature of the network into Community[16].

3. However, the experience of Community is also a "logical experience", that is to say, an intellectual, philosophical and political-discovery that can be shared. Exchanges, testimonies, readings, philosophy and social sciences offer a possible access to this reality by way of transmission. Thus, Community is lived but also deduced from the information that circulates (stories, œuvres, conversations, etc.). Community is object of transmission and, in a way, also of "initiations" that is simply operated by socialisation and culture. In the absence of or in the continuation of an immediate significant experience (through the "voice" of the arts or by way of the aforementioned ecstatic experience), Community is susceptible to mediated experiences in which the vectors are here again concrete and unmistakable traces of its existence. In this sense, all works of philosophy, sociology, or politics dedicated to the Community also testify to its existence. Not so much because they would materially contribute in delineating the contours and making it exist as an object of "dispute" (as ANT conceives of the somewhat "configuring" trace that sociologists leave of their object of study), but rather because the experience of the Community is effectively transmitted through the human mind.

We will have understood that there is much evidence – that satisfy ANT's laudable concerns for rationality and objectivity – indicating the importance of not considering Community as a pure "illusion" of the sociologist. We must conclude then that maintaining this notion is both desirable and necessary in view of a rich and complex understanding of the social in general, or even of associations of actors within a network.

---

[16] A myriad of localised experiences (for example, from the Commune of Paris to the ZAD of Notre-Dame-des-Landes) testify to the Community and to the power of its "presence". For recent examples of testimony, see those compiled by the "Mauvaise troupe" collective in *Constellations, trajectoires révolutionnaires pour le jeune XXIᵉ siècle*.

Conclusion

If the question of the maintenance of this notion could legitimately be posed and the seed of doubt be sewn, owing to the developments of this radical ANT sociology, it is that, contrary to what existed in the past, we are nowadays experiencing the social like we experience Community: by its *lack*. It is with this bias that we all experience at the most quotidian level what we in fact call the "social". The sense of belonging has entered a crisis, writes Latour (2005: 13). He adds: "We are no longer sure about what 'we' means; we seem to be bound by 'ties' that don't look like regular social ties. Thus, the overall project of what we are supposed to do together is thrown into doubt." Yet, this development, which justified the approach of returning to a strict "realism" in ANT, concerns society but not Community! If both are now invisible, what differentiates the experience of society from that of Community is that the former has become an extremely tenuous and vaporous experience, whereas the latter has always been an extremely strong experience, even if ephemeral.

The renewed sociology proposed by ANT (that of a new description of "assemblages")[17] is itself inseparable from a new formulation of the definition of society: it would gain to be understood, Latour says, as "… *a fluid* visible only when new associations are being made" (*Changer de société*: 113). We easily understand how this new definition can in fact more effectively account for the observations of ANT sociologists and, perhaps, new social realities as well. It turns out that indeed this "fluid" concept carries with it many signifiers that are well suited to the description of the "new" social. Nonetheless, it is not clear if is always in the sense that Latour had in mind in proposing this definition. Such is the definition of fluid according to the dictionary:

1. "That which flows without a fixed form" and, as we have noted, this is evidently an essential characteristic of our liquid modernity (Bauman). It is also one of the fundamental contributions of ANT, which emphasises the *movement* of the social against conceptions that define it as fixed and sedimented;

2. "That which, without form, takes the form of its container [gas, liquid]." Here indeed is a definition that effectively characterises

---

[17] As it is expressly formulated in title of the English-language edition: *Reassembling the Social.*

the *network* of which all the social would ultimately be composed of.
3. However, it is in the third sense of the word – that of a subtle influence – that we find what is most interesting in the choice of the term:
4. "Force, subtle and mysterious influence, that emanates from the
stars, beings or things."
5. Here, at the conclusion of this analysis, we return to that in which
the actor-network sociology precisely built itself against: the idea
of a non-material force that nonetheless determines material
forms, to mysterious entelechies that govern the social. We cannot
but agree with this understanding of the "fluidity of the social";
for this *influence* is precisely the very force of Community, its calling, the way in which it manifests and the form its presence takes
in the world.

Ultimately, it would seem that the logic of ANT cannot help but
recover – and validate – the spiritual dimension, not strictly observable,
to which it claimed to be initially opposed. With a description of the
social that is characterised as "fluctuating" (movement and network), it
opens the door to an understanding that is less radically flat and imma-
nent than it would have imagined. By its empiricism, it introduces *in fine*
the possibility of the Community as an acting force, whose presence is
as subtle as its effect undeniable. Finally, an *affect*, a communal affect,
as a mode of affectation of the actors; creator of ties, and thus, yes, of a
network that in the end colours the Community with a power of attach-
ment that the radical version of the actor-network sociology was not supposed to recognise.

Though we must critique this theory, we can also see by virtue of its
rigour, how it can better help us to think of Community. It invites us in
particular to understand what it is that we seek to designate under this
term and, most importantly, to understand a *process* of communisation
that *valorises* a particular link between actors – the communal tie. Thus,
Community is better understood as a form of *shared existential experience*
(communion) that provokes the desire to recover this "quality of relation"
and thus becomes a force that shapes social relations. It still remains for
us, following the precepts of ANT, to specify the modes of presence of
this force. For our part, it would consist in following the analysis that
began some years ago on the aesthetics of the common[18], that is to say,

---

[18]   After a first symposium on the "Images of the Common" (2016), a second on
"The words of the Common and of the Community" (2018), we look forward to a

on the way in which Community "tells itself" through works of art. By means of a refined understanding of these mechanisms, it will perhaps become possible, not to reform sociology but, in the least, the perception of the role of aesthetics in social interactions.

References

Agamben Giorgio, *La communauté qui vient*, Paris, Seuil, 1990.

Astruc Rémi, *Nous? L'aspiration à la Communauté et les arts*, Versailles, RKI Press, 2016.

Comité Invisible, *À nos amis*, Paris, La Fabrique, 2014.

Latour Bruno, *Pasteur. Bataille contre les microbes*, Paris, Nathan, 1985.

Latour Bruno, *Changer de société, refaire de la sociologie*, Paris, La Découverte, 2005.

Latour Bruno, *Enquête sur les modes d'existence*, Paris, La Découverte, 2012.

Latour Bruno, *Le Travail des sociétés*, Paris, Seuil, 2009.

Latour Bruno, *Où atterrir? Comment s'orienter en politique*, Paris, La Découverte, 2019a.

Latour Bruno, *Face à Gaïa: Huit conférences sur le nouveau régime climatique*, Paris, La Découverte, 2019b.

Maniglier Patrice, "Institution symbolique et vie sémiologique: la réalité sociale des signes chez Durkheim et Saussure", in *Revue de métaphysique et de morale*, no. 54, 2007, p. 179–204.

Nancy Jean-Luc (avec Bailly J.-C.), *La Comparution*, Paris, Christian Bourgois, 1991.

Tönnies Ferdinand, *Communauté et société*, Paris, PUF, 2010.

Vibert Stéphane, "La Référence à la société come 'Totalité'. Pour un réalisme ontologique de l'être-en-société", in *Société* no. 26, Autumn 2006, p. 79–113.

Vibert Stéphane, "Le bain acide des relations de pouvoir. Critique de la socio-anthropologie potestative", in *Revue du MAUSS*, 2016/1, no. 47, p. 287–303.

Weber Max, *Les communautés*, Paris, La Découverte, 2019.

third series entitled "Gestures, rhythms, movements of the Common" (upcoming in 2022).

Messianism and community[1]

Antonin Chambon

Translated by Phoebe Chetwynd and Tara Ostiguy

You tell me, Prince Adam, that you can find no thread. You can see none so long as you are willing to try nothing less than the disentanglement of the whole. The beginning and the beginning alone is placed into the hands of men [...]. Simply make a beginning and at once you will see all about you, in the very circle of your personal activity, all kinds of threads. You will have to grasp but a single one of them and it will be, if God wills it, the right one.

Maggid of Konitz to Adam Czartoryski, Prince of Poland.
Martin Buber, *Gog and Magog*

Why should we return to consider a thousand-year-old tradition and a thought as elaborate and specific as that of Jewish messianism to enrich contemporary reflections on the community? Today, there is a proliferation of debates, both in contemporary philosophy and politics, on the dissolution or the necessary renewal of the community and the *common*. Should they not rightly wipe the slate clean of old ideas which no longer seem relevant to our reflections on the shared space of our emancipated societies? Faced with such questions, we would like to show that the messianic thought that developed at different times in the Jewish tradition may be able to enrich, perhaps even with a certain relevance, our contemporary reflections on the community and the common as

---

[1] This article represents the very first steps towards a broader study on the notion of messianism and community in the thought of E. Levinas and W. Benjamin. We can in no way claim here an expert and elaborate analysis of the question of messianism in the Jewish tradition. In this regard, this text seeks above all to articulate and situate a problem, as well as to indicate, in the closing remarks of the article, the direction that we would like to follow in the development of this work towards a potential resolution.

both an operator and a conceptual tool. Here, we will lay out only the foundations for such an intuition, for a study of the present informed by thoughts that are ancient yet still alive and which, we hope, can justify the relevance of this research.

It should first of all be emphasised that, at first glance, messianic consciousness does not have a significant presence in the biblical corpus, strictly speaking. Rather, it arises historically within Jewish tradition largely in the form of apocalyptic messianism (Scholem 2011: 1–36). According to G. Scholem, in reaction to disastrous historical events such as the second destruction of the Temple of Jerusalem or the expulsion of the Jews from Spain in 1492, ancient prophesies were reinterpreted that reinforced a notion of apocalyptic messianism that would occur in two-stages. Here, the two facets of the Messiah were represented as the "son of Joseph", which stirs awareness of future catastrophes and previously unimaginable cataclysms, and the "son of David", which corresponds to the utopian aspect of messianic times. The first opens the way to the unfolding of the second, where messianic utopia must immediately be grasped as justice inside a political horizon. Indeed – and this is perhaps the greatest contrast with Christian messianism – redemption can only come about as a public act, addressed to the whole community and never only to one man's solitary heart. Messianic utopia can then be understood as a liberation of the community, the unfolding of its own potentiality and the reign of justice – as much within itself as in its relationship to other communities. In this respect, it should be emphasised that the peaceful coexistence between messianism and the Halakha[2] could often only be maintained if messianic expectation did not occupy a strong and affective presence, as this would unleash, in the eyes of the Halakah itself, the dangerous possibilities of antinomic and anarchic behaviour (Scholem 2011: 49–77). Moreover, the rabbinical authorities, having to account for the social and political calm of Jewish communities, might have sought to defend a messianic expectation that was foremost fideistic in order to diminish possible revolutionary impulses.

Today, we face the challenges of a prevailing contemporary discourse that emphasises the imminence of a general collapse – at once democratic,

---

[2]   Halakha is often translated by "Jewish law". It is a collective body of text based on the written Torah and the Talmudic and rabbinic law. It expresses not only the religious practices and beliefs but also, to certain extent, some aspects of the day-to-day life.

economic and ecological – as well as the possibility it could engender for the reinvention of community practices. This highly affective discourse paints the possibility of a dystopian utopia and living through and beyond a collapse so radical that it cannot even be assimilated. It dictates that we will have to seize upon the occasion, despite the present catastrophe (and perhaps even because of it), to rediscover a relationship to the Other – human or non-human – that is both just and free[3]. In light of such contemporary discourses, might we not wonder how our reflections upon such a situation might be enriched by a tradition as rich in thought and community experiences as that of Jewish messianism?

In order to better understand how messianic thought could revive reflections on the community beyond our usual approach to such a notion, we would first like to take up again the problematic of the community which is at hand.

Community and totality: "The work of death" and the appearance of alterity

We should therefore consider in depth our present anxiety about all ideas of the community which are based *a priori* on the sharing of a common or on a characteristic shared by each of its members – or thus established by the very act of founding the community. In other words, an anxiety about a community that would be based on a logic of unification. To return to the analysis of Jean-Luc Nancy in his famous article "The Inoperative Community" in *Aléas*, this approach to the community – whose movement is grasped by Nancy through an analysis of communist totalitarianisms but which could be extended to a more general conception of community – would find its fulfilment in the Christian ideal of *communion*. That is to say, a tendency towards totalisation and unification which is likened to a process of *digestion* of alterity, a tendency that Nancy designates as "immanentism" (Nancy 2012: 1–42).

The community is understood first of all as the sharing of a particularity (a work, a *praxis*, a biological or cultural trait etc.,) which

---

[3]   See, among other publications, the popularisation of such a discourse in the editorial success that was Pablo Servigne's *Une autre fin du monde est possible. Vivre l'effondrement (et pas seulement y survivre)*.

ultimately comes to define this community and the identity of its members. At first sight, the members seem to be nothing other than this identity. Thus, we speak of the Jewish, gay, proletarian communities, etc., and their members as a Jew, a gay person, a proletarian etc. Yet in the identity that is created by this shared particularity, the singularity of its members is reduced. The singular is precisely that which does not form a community, that which stands alone in a primary difference *vis-à-vis* others. As soon as it is absorbed within a community, this singularity is redefined according to the common identity and its intrinsic otherness is placed outside the community – that is to say, outside of *that which is common*. There is indeed an opposition between a singular identity and a community identity.

Finally, the notion of the community would see its ultimate unfolding in the hegemony of this established common identity. The ideal and completed horizon would be that of a community where this established common is total. That which is not common is not, strictly speaking, a matter for the community. It is eventually tolerated but it must never take precedence over that which is common in the identity of the person. If this "negative part", this singular which cannot be absorbed into the Same, were to take precedence in defining the identity of each member, then it would come to jeopardise the unity of the community and precisely its nature as a community. In other words, to realise a community is to collapse all differences into a common. Once realised, the community is *one* within itself. Thus, we understand how the community is by definition stretched towards communion and fusion, in that it is in this communion that the totality of its movement would be achieved[4].

Now, this definition first of all poses a logical problem with the very concept of community. In fact, a community presupposes a difference – at least minimal – between its members so that the establishment of a common can take place. In the same way that the unity of a musical chord relies upon the friction between the vibrations of each of its notes,

---

[4]   And yet, the complete abandonment of the concept of community is impossible. There has to be community, if only for there to be a world, a space that could receive my subjectivity and that of another in a sharing. Without anything in common, we would be in the absurdity of a world which would be either a desert, a solitude where nothing makes sense for someone other than me, or a chaos of ever-changing differences in which we could not progress for lack of a *something* to progress in, a common space.

that space that exists between each member is a condition of possibility for the community. This fusion towards which the notion of the community tends would then be both its completion and its dissolution, the ruin of its first condition of possibility. It is no longer possible to say that there is community since we no longer distinguish, in their singularities, the entities that compose it. The relationship of the same to the same cannot form a community. In other words, the community contains within its own logic that which prevents it from existing, its own impossibility.

In Nancy's analysis, this poses an ethical and ontological problem. If it is a question here of approaching the singularity of each being as an obstacle to the unfolding of the common; and if a being is, according to Nancy's thesis, *always* singular, then the process of completion of such a community would unfold in the passage from what *is* – the singularity – to what *is not* – the Same. That which Nancy then calls "the work of death" of "immanentism", is a term which we must understand both as an untenable ontological paradox, as well as the potentially effective death of singular beings themselves (Nancy 2012: 1–42).

Thus, it is in response to this logical, ontological and ethical problem that messianic thought can provide a rich and radical reflection, from which could develop different approaches to a community that is understood otherwise than in its totalising logic. First, messianism proper must be disassociated from its secularisation in modern thought on History. From this point of view, an eschatology appears that is much more radical than that of philosophies of progress[5]. It is not at all the culmination of a dialectical and historical process which would come, at the end of time, to grasp the twists and turns of History and to justify them in light of its completion. As if History gestated itself and that its completion would see the revelation of its truth in a necessary historical utopia. It would then only be a matter of tracking the dialectical process of historical time which – inevitable and in a way comprehensible to the human mind – would result in the redemption of human suffering within the ideal of justice. Here, the end of history would come to justify the means – and the potential suffering that these means could cause. In opposition to this process and the relief that it offers from the ruins of history through a final, necessary and rational utopia, messianism proposes a much more radical and abrupt emergence. In no case can the

---

[5]   Here, we are following the arguments of G. Bensussan (2001a).

advent of messianic times in the Jewish tradition be understood as the result of historical times, as the march of men towards progress of any kind. It is always a divine act, a decision left to God himself, that is to say, to the highest Alterity which is impossible to assimilate (Scholem 2011: 1–36). Thus, messianism signals the unpredictable emergence of a time that is completely other, which would come not to justify History but to ruin it. Although there are varying positions on the matter of messianic "impatience" with regard to the desire to "hasten the end", it is nonetheless never a question of acting directly and historically to bring about the coming of messianic times. It is thus that messianism carries within itself a highly radical conception of both the collapse of the world and the arising of a utopia. It is not simply a suspension of the totality and its logic but rather the ruin of the totality itself.

Messianic awaiting could therefore be the core around which – and from which – the community comes to form. No longer based on a positively shared common but on an absence – that is to say, on the possibility of the emergence of the most radical otherness, the gesture of an Other, the decree of a God that can in no way be assimilated by mankind under a logic of totalisation. Messianism presents a mode of rupture which, as we have seen, must be grasped immediately within a political perspective of the liberation of the community and of its relations. The question is therefore that of the messianic awaiting itself, that of knowing under which modality it would allow the realisation of a community which is not, in and of itself, *resistance* to the logic of the common and of totalisation but, in fact, *the ruin* of this very logic. And so, what could "awaiting messianic times" mean for us who wish to think and live, at present, a community that has Otherness at its heart?

"Let the Messiah come, but may I not see him" (Sanhedrin 98b)

We would therefore like to investigate different forms of messianic expectation in order to better understand how they could be bearers of a community-building force whose dynamism would be outside of any totalising logic. Faced with catastrophes to come that we would like to understand as the "birth pangs" of the Messiah and his utopia, what could be our position in this awaiting? Do we have the slightest role to play here or are we constrained to a passive and yet faithful waiting for the redemption that will undoubtedly come one day?

In this regard, it should first of all be noted that apocalyptic messianism may have been received with suspicion on the part of certain rationalist rabbinical movements, to the extent of wanting to dismiss its apocalyptic aspects that are literally extra-ordinary. In the *Mishneh Torah*, Maimonides indeed affirms "It should not occur to you that during the days of the Messiah a single thing from the 'ways of the world' will be cancelled nor will there be something novel in the Creation. Rather, the world will continue in its customary way" (Maimonides, Michnè Torah: 1)[6]. Here is a matter of eliminating potential political and ethical disruptions which could be triggered by the declaration of Messianic time before its actual arrival, as well as to guard against the blasphemy of a human declaration of the end of exile. Messianic utopia is therefore understood only as political peace and the realisation of a purely contemplative ideal: "The Sages and Prophets did not long for the days of the Messiah because they wanted to rule the world [...]. Rather, they desired this so that they would have time for Torah and its Wisdom. [...]. At that time there will be no famines and no wars, no envy and no competition [...]. The world will only be engaged in knowing God" (Mamonides: 4–5). Thus, Maimonides defends a messianic waiting that is above all fideistic. A coming of the Messiah in which we must believe without ever trying to hasten the coming and which must be rid of any overly strong utopian character which would come to destroy or endanger the laws of the Halakah: "The twelfth principle [of the Jewish faith, on the Messianic era,] is to believe and to confirm that he will come and not to think that he is late." "If the tarries, wait for him" and do not give him a [set] time and do not create analyses from the verses to extrapolate the time of his coming. And the sages said, "The spirit of those that calculate the end should blow up" (Maimonides, Commentary, Introduction). Although we cannot reduce the rationalist position of Maimonides to that of a passive messianism (A. Funkenstein, 2007)[7], we see here the

---

[6]   If we follow the research of A. Funkenstein in *Nature, histoire et messianisme*, this passage would by no means be a rejection of messianism. It was precisely because the messianic times were near, according to Maimonides, that such distrust in the face of the apocalyptic aspects of messianism would be justified.

[7]   Thus the question of rabbinical ordination (*semikha*) in the *Commentary on the Michna* could have been used to justify certain attempts "to smooth the way of the Messiah" by referring to Maimonides when he affirms there, "I think that the

neutralisation of its utopian force. Through this rationalist position and a "restorative" messianism, Maimonides urges less the creation of new communities than the deepening of the study of the Halakha and its own ethics (Scholem 2011: 1–36).

Despite the fundamental importance of Maimonides' position, the latter does not present the final answer to the question of Messianic waiting. Indeed, there are different messianic "crises" in Jewish history – which Maimonides precisely seeks to stymie – in which a more vivid creative force is unveiled when it comes to community experiences. We would therefore like to direct our attention to a kind of paradoxical messianic activism that appeared between the 16th and 17th centuries.

In response to the Expulsion from Spain in 1492 – one of the most significant destructions in Western Jewish history – we see over the course of the next three generations, the emergence of the School of Safed and of the second Kabbalah that revolves around the figures of Moses Cordovero and Isaac Luria. We see here a particular reinterpretation of the first Spanish Kabbalah which, in direct reaction to the ongoing Expulsion, would reintegrate messianic and apocalyptic elements that had not been central to the first Kabbalists (Scholem 1946, 2001: 48–141). Thus developed a rich and complex theology and cosmology around three fundamental notions: the *Tzimtzum*, the *Shevirat Ha-Kelim* and the *Tikkun*[8]. According to G. Sholem's analyses on this topic, one can see in Safed's Kabbalah the elaboration of a cosmological myth of Exile. The *Tzimtzum* is the first movement: God contracts within himself in order to liberate a space in which creation can take place. The first act of creation therefore becomes the withdrawal of God *into himself*. Exile is then understood on the basis of this withdrawal and thus takes on an ontological characteristic which will then apply to the whole of creation. The notion of *Tikkun* then – which can be translated by repair or restoration – concerns the process which would restore the

---

Sanhedrin will be restored before the revelation of the Messiah, it will even be one of the portentous signs of the imminence of his coming; as it says "I will restore the judges as in the old days" (Is. 1,26) (Maimonides, Commentary, I, 3).

[8]   Here, we will focus only on the notion of the *Tikkun* although this is an arbitrary and schematic separation because the three concepts form an organic whole. To consider these concepts as a whole would take us outside the limits of our subject. The choice is also justified because of the importance of the *Tikkun* to the renewal of contemporary ideas of the community as demonstrated in the journal by the same name (*Tiqqun*) and the practical continuities that have been drawn from it.

first unity of being and release the sparks of the first divine light that were scattered and imprisoned in creation[9]. G. Scholem points out that for the School of Safed, "[the *Tikkun*] is the task of every one of us [...]. From this soul of all souls [that of the first Adam, *Adam Kadmon*, from which the divine light is divided], sparks have scattered in all directions and become diffused into matter. The problem is to reassemble them, to lift them to their proper place and to restore the spiritual nature of man in its original splendor" (*ibid.*). In other words, *Tikkun* is a cosmic process, a significant part of which belongs to the *creature* more than the Creator himself. Responsibility for its completion rests upon man and his actions. "Certain parts of the process of restitution are allotted to man [...]. Every act of man is related to this final task which God has set for His creatures" (*ibid.*). For Luria, *Tikkun* is, strictly speaking, a continuous process, the completion of which is none other than the appearance of the Messiah. It is to say that *Tikkun* is indeed a messianic process, certain actions of which are the responsibility of man. There is therefore a vast expansion of messianic responsibility and we can see how such a doctrine could – in contrast to the first Spanish Kabbalah – have had a very wide popular influence. Indeed "formerly [the *Galuth*, the Exile] had been regarded either as a punishment for Israel's sins or as a test of Israel's faith. Now it still is all this, but intrinsically it is a mission: its purpose is to uplift the fallen sparks from all their various locations" (*ibid.*). It is a matter here of each man participating in the messianic adventure of the advent of the Redemption, and in the ethical and political utopia which accompanies it.

Such a valorisation of individual action could not but have a significant impact on the *lived experience* of messianic expectation and the intensity of men's desire for a redemption to come. Without necessarily making a causal relationship between the emergence of the Kabbalah of Safed and the messianic event of the Sabbatian movement, we can still argue that the sudden popularity of this movement could no doubt have thrived on the doctrine of the *Tikkun* and the elevation of sparks specific to this school[10]. In this way, the appearance of Sabbatai Zevi,

---

[9] This is obviously a considerable and allusive reduction of the Kabbalistic doctrine of "the rise of sparks" and its cosmogonic myth. We will not go into details on such processes here, despite its fascinating and rich aspects, because it would take us too far from our subject (see Scholem: 1946).

[10] Indeed, after the apostasy of the Messiah, we observe an elaborate attempt to justify his conversion to Islam by arguing that it was his duty to free the sparks from the

forty years after the death of Isaac Luria, finds fertile ground on which to deploy the force, both creative and destructive, of a messianic time *that has come* and thus gives rise to many new communities. The speed with which the "reign" of Sabbatai Zevi unfolds would suggest that a vivid messianic expectation, spurred by the political troubles of the time, become a messianic *impatience*, seizing upon the opportunity provided by the present moment to declare the beginning of the redemption and the end of Exile. From this moment on, we observe the proliferation of Sabbatian communities that will embody a force of theological invention and an antinomic, almost anarchic, power of great magnitude. It should be noted that the development of the Sabbatian communities would survive long after the apostasy of their Messiah, which took place only a year after his recognition (Scholem 2011: 49–77). One could see here a completely "counterfactual" fulfilment of messianic times and its utopia. That is to say, none of the characteristics traditionally recognised in messianic times are found to be truly reunited in this period. The apostasy of Sabbatai Zevi denies both the traditional figure of the Messiah and the disappearance of persecutions; no war is waged and the reunion of the people of Israel is far from having taken place. This will lead "believers" to experience a real opposition between their inner revelation – that of the liberation of messianic times – and the external events of the world. Thus, it opens the door to an antinomical reinterpretation of tradition and the Halakah, making Sabbatianism one of the greatest heresies in Jewish history.

However, these communities born of such a messianic impatience did not so much aim at the destruction of the traditional laws as at a total reversal of them. For the radical wing of Sabbatianism, it was less a matter of asserting an exit from the Halakah than of justifying its own antinomism through the Halakah (Scholem 2011: 78–141). Since messianic times lead to an eternal Shabbat, some branches of the Sabbatian movement argued that the sanctity of the laws governing the world before the redemption would now be found overturned and it would be a sin to follow them. This is evidenced by Sabbatai Zevi's reinterpretation of the blessing of the morning prayer from "Blessed art Thou O Lord [...] who freest those who are in bondage [*mattir asurim*]" to "Blessed art Thou O Lord [...] who permittest the forbidden [*mattir isurim*], who permits that

---

Kelipoth, and therefore to plunge into the evil forces in order to release the pieces of divine light which constitutes evil's life-giving force.

which is forbidden" (Scholem 2011: 78–141) Thus, in the Dönmeh community of Salonica, we see the establishment of "the extinction of lights", an orgiastic rite of exchange of women (A. Galanté 1986: 169–292). Furthermore, in the extreme case of Baruchiah Russo, we see not only the lifting of the ban on incest but also the encouragement of incest as a positive precept of the new Messianic Torah (Scholem 2011). Eventually, these communities would evolve in closed circles, often keeping their new practices of Judaism hidden by converting to another monotheism, and would eventually centralise around authoritarian and charismatic figures. This can be seen in the Dönmeh community revolving around Baruchiah Russo, in the Frankists, and in the mythical elaboration of the figure of Sabbatai Zevi.

However, one can wonder about what seems to be the stumbling block of this revived messianic consciousness and its creative utopian power. The Sabbatian movement seems to be a possible response to messianic impatience and to the desire to see the time of redemption and the realisation of its communities in present time. It is now a matter of looking more in depth at this notion of impatience and seeing how it is intrinsically linked to the figure that is conferred on the Messiah. If in this figure we see a man coming to liberate creation and wage needed messianic wars, how does this dictate the affectivity of waiting and thereby the impatience that arises? Could the abandonment of this figure open a way to another understanding and another satisfaction of messianic impatience that does not take the risks of the Sabbatian path? Indeed, if we are to believe G. Bensussan in *The Messianic Time*, "we may not even know what it is to wait if we only wait for a revelation or a *Parousia* [coming, presence]" (Bensussan 2001: 15–32, my translation).

"Today, if you hear his voice" (Ps. 95,7)

We would like then to focus on a passage from the Sanhedrin Treaty, in 98a. It is said that Rabbi Yehoshua ben Levi one day met the prophet Elijah at the entrance to a cave. Rabbi Yehoshua asks him, "when will the Messiah come?" to which Elijah responds: "Go and ask Him." When the Rabbi asks him where to find the Messiah and how to recognise Him, the prophet replies "He is at the gates of Rome, sitting with the poor who suffer from illnesses. All of them untie and retie their bandages all at once, but He unties and reties one bandage at a time, saying: "When I will be called upon to bring about the Redemption, above all I must not be delayed by redoing my dressings." The Talmud tells that Rabbi Yehoshua went to Rome and among the poor in need he meets the Messiah. Then he asks the Messiah, "when will you come, Master?" "Today", responds the Messiah to the great joy of the Rabbi. However, the day passes and the Messiah does not come. The Rabbi returns to Elijah and complains: "He did not speak the truth to me, He lied, He said He would come today, and He did not come!" Elijah replies, "that is exactly what He said to you: Today, *if you hear His voice* (Ps. 97, 7)". Thus, ends the story of this meeting.

What does such a story tell us? What is at stake in such a reversal of the messianic advent and of the coming redemption? For it is no longer a matter of waiting for a Messiah who would come to end historical time and allay the sufferings of creation; who would come from the outside to save us. Here it is the Messiah himself who awaits man, always ready to come "if you hear His voice". And this waiting no longer takes place in an other-worldly space which he would leave to reveal himself and offer us redemption. Instead, he is "at the gates of Rome", right there in the world and in its suffering, a suffering that is precisely caused by this waiting. It is no longer a question, then, of an eschatological messianism which would come at the "end of time", of an end point which would come to conclude the chronological arrow, of a rupture which would demarcate a before and an after in the time of Exile. Such a story seems instead to take us from a messianic *awaiting* to an *attention* to the messianicity of the present, to the redeeming richness of each instant and to the act that falls to us – that of attentive listening to the possible redemption contained in the presentness of the world. It is a messianism of the moment, always already there, waiting and, in the suffering of this waiting, always ready to be heard, ready for man to finally turn his attention to the possible immediacy of redemption. As Rosenzweig pointed out "[there is] the *today* that is merely a bridge to tomorrow and the *today* that is a springboard to eternity." It would seem that it is a question here of understanding *today* as such a springboard. To break the linearity of chronological time to taste the fecundity of the moment, the eternity that hides in it, and the redemption of suffering that could unfold from it.

Finally, it is indeed a whole relationship to time which finds itself turned upside down by this "messianism of the event" (Bensussan 2001: 15–32). The Messiah stands before us no longer as an awaited future but as always already here. The possibility of redemption is therefore no longer in a future whose end could be calculated but rather in a past and a present whose suffering is waiting to be heard. Thus, we distance ourselves from messianism conceived as a coming utopia and as a catastrophe that will announce and permit redemption – all still understood within a "history" whose end is near – to give place to a redemption that is summoned in the immediacy of present time. Following the analysis of G. Bensussan, it is a matter here of abandoning the concept of an objectifiable time which would not be *beforehand* lived in first person. To objectify time would always be to bring it back to a spatialised conception, to a line or a circle on which a series of equivalent seconds can be written (*ibid*.: 37–45). But time, as an "element in which we have the intuition of ourselves", always overflows the framework of its spatialisation. Here, such a "messianism of the event" would come to seize this overflow in order to restore the primacy of a time lived in first person: a past which faces us and a future into which we advance backwards, an indeterminable future since it is always dependent on our listening to the fecundity of the present[11]. A messianic consciousness which reveals a temporal interpenetration and which "captures all the relationships by which a subject takes place, from his own situation, in the network of generations, births and deaths [...] that is to say, in history, in Hebrew *toledot*, engenderings" (*ibid*.: 37–45, my translation).

This upheaval in the relation to time, which stems from a messianic attention to each instant, appears closer to Benjamin's interruption of time and to the radical ethics of Levinas. In other words, it offers the possibility of understanding messianism as a rupture of the world *and* as the immediacy of the relation to the Other.

Indeed, facing a past that summons us while being projected into an always unknown future, feeling this desire to interrupt the march of time in order to testify to its ruins, is this not the exact position in which Benjamin's Angel of History finds himself, caught in the storm of progress?

> His face is turned towards the past. Where we see the appearance of a chain of events, he sees one single catastrophe [...]. He would like to pause for a

---

[11] G. Bensussan points out that where the Indo-European languages establish a quasi-equivalence between front and future, behind and past, the Hebrew *qadam* means before and past (time of origins), and *akhor*, behind, designates the outcome, the end of an era and a future that only presents itself as a blind horizon.

moment, to awaken the dead and to piece together what has been smashed. But a storm is blowing from Paradise, it has caught itself up in his wings [...] The storm drives him irresistibly into the future, to which his back is turned, while the rubble-heap before him grows sky-high. That which we call progress, is this storm (Benjamin 1940).

Now, the Angel's desire, the desire of stopping time "[to] awaken the dead and make whole what has been smashed", is it not also that messianic attention whose necessity is revealed to us by Psalm 95,7 "Today if you hear His voice?" And is it not ultimately that which Benjamin designates as "weak messianic power?"

> The past carries a secret index with it, by which it is referred to its resurrection [...]. Is there not an echo of those who have been silenced in the voices to which we lend our ears today? [...] If so, then there is a secret appointment between the generations of the past and that of our own. For we have been expected upon this earth. For it has been given us to know, just like every generation before us, a weak messianic power, on which the past has a claim (Benjamin 1940).

This "weak messianic power" that only reveals itself in a time lived in the first person, in which the redeeming fecundity of the moment is felt, appears to be understood as an ethical imperative towards the Other. That is to say, an imperative to face the suffering of these past lives and of those who suffer today and who, precisely by their nature of being in suffering, always reveal an irreducible gap between the Other and the Self. This opens the way to the structure of Levinasian ethics, that of a diachronic time and of a relationship with the Other which is never that of a presence but always that of an absence that calls out to us.

G. Bensussan emphasises that "[messianic] time is a way of relating to the other, or to the infinite, without *ever* being able to appropriate it [...] a way of relating to it, however, *in* the same, *in* the finite" (Bensussan 2001: 94–104). In other words, messianic time is the very way in which the Face of the Other appears to me, unassimilable and yet an uncompromising call for help. It is also the way in which ethics, while dwelling beyond being and the totality, has no other way to meet this call than through *being* itself. If ethics for Levinas is a rupture of the world of "economy" and self-interest – a realm of *being* understood as *conatus essendi* – it nevertheless requires this world so that the gift may transpire, so that being "torn up from oneself for another in the giving to the other of the bread out of ones own mouth" (Levinas 2004: 220–222) can take place. This ambivalence specific to the ethical relationship, that of a flickering between what always exceeds my power and what nonetheless calls for my sacrifice, is understood here as "weak messianic power".

In the Messiah's response to Rabbi Yehoshua, the voice in question then becomes a cry, a cry for conscience to be born and revealed inside our consciousness and for both to merge together. "[To] hear His voice" becomes this effort of conscience that falls to man and on which "the past has a claim". The messianic possibility would be found there. The utopia of a suffering that is heard and to which man responds in action (Levinas 2005: 65–110)[12], claiming no pretension to comprehension and making no attempt to bring it back to *my* experience. That is to say: abandoning the return to the Self. And thus, ruin of self-interest, collapse of the other as an object of the world from which I could profit (even if only to gain a good conscience), collapse of the Self as a movement of totalisation and digestion of Otherness, and end to the Odyssean adventure of a return to oneself. The "weak messianic power" would play out in the listening of conscience and in the action which ensues from this. It would be in the letting of this conscience direct the actions of man face to the Other that participation in the messianic adventure and the ruin of the world of self-interest could unfold. Does not Hebrew draw *matspoun*, conscience, together with compass, *matzpen*, that which indicates the way?

It is thus an ethics which would no longer be based on the recognition of *my* own kind but rather on that of his otherness. That is to say, the ruin of the logic of the common and of the Same, and yet a modality of the relation to the Other. Can we now re-read the notion of *Tikkun* – this participation of man in the messianic adventure, in the ending of an ontological Exile – as violence done to the Self and ethical action face to the suffering of the Other? According to Martin Buber, this is what 18th century Polish Hassidism puts into practice, which he himself calls "Kabbalism made Ethics". "The elevation of divine sparks", dispersed into creation, calls for the performance of an ethical action in rupture with the world. And thus, it calls for a continuous redemption: "only the hallowing of all actions without distinction... possesses redemptive power. Only out

---

12   Levinas often refers to Isaiah 6, 8 "here I am, send me" in *Otherwise than being, or, Beyond essence*, as the very figure of subjectivity. Faced with the Face of the Other, subjectivity first appears as an accusative case (the answer: "here I am") before being a nominative subject. But this "here I am" immediately means "send me", a gift of the self in the world and in ethical action. See also Levinas, and his commentary on *Shabbat* 88 a-b, specifically the phrase "They did before hearing" (Levinas 2005).

of the redemption of the everyday does the All-Day of redemption grow" (Buber 1960: 107). But the *Tikkun* sees the exile as the ontological state of creation and no longer only that of man. It is Being as a whole which is revealed as this Other whose Face calls out to me and to which I have no choice but to respond. The *Tikkun*, as an ethical *and* ontological restoration, is not limited to the human other but opens out to all that exists. It is all that surrounds man then that calls to be heard as "Face", Alterity in suffering, and whose redemption falls to me.

Messianism can therefore be understood no longer as a utopia to come after the ruin of History, but rather as an interruption *in present time* of the totalisation of the Self, of this movement which endlessly seeks to bring the Other back into the Same. Therefore, a relationship to the Other is revealed, which receives its otherness as such, and is extended to the whole of Being. If messianism can be understood as such, what community could unfold from this consciousness – that which has the radicality of conscience at its core? We know that Levinas deploys ethics politically only in a logic of the State, and that Benjamin conceives of messianism as a violence even more radical than any founding or contesting violence (Benjamin 2000). Would it be possible then, through the interrupting violence of Benjamin's "weak messianic power" – understood as attention to the suffering of the Other – to deploy the Levinassian ethics, no longer in the logic of a State but in that of a community, which would confer upon it a radicality of ethics and a radical break with world politics? What community can be informed by such a messianism of the present and its ethical rupture?

Community and messianism

Here, the aim is only to indicate lines of thought and inspiration that we would like to deepen in order to seek an understanding of community which is no longer thought of under the logic of the common, of resemblance and of assimilation. We have seen how such a logic could lead the community to unfold as the incorporation of otherness, digestion of singularity and ultimately potential "work of death" within a common and unified identity. How then to think the community so that it is not simply resistance to this logic, but rather the ruin of it; that is to say, a reception of the singularity and affectivity of the Self facing the Other that is so radical that no return to the self could be possible?

Thus, we think that Judaism's thought on messianism, as a philosophical tool, could enrich these reflections and inform us about certain risks and possibilities of contemporary thought on the community. We have proposed an understanding of messianism, which rests upon a coming catastrophe and a personalised figure of the Messiah, that would always incur the risk of closing itself too quickly around this very figure and, in wanting to take a stand against an obsolete world, could finally only grow in a simple relationship of inversion to it. Thus, when faced with such a risk, we have argued that a fideist messianism is not the only answer as its call for an awaiting is perhaps too passive to bear within it a creative force towards the renewal of communities. Instead, through a "messianism of the event" and an ethical listening, we can find a rupture of a world which takes place within the world itself; no longer a messianic awaiting but an attention to the messianism of the moment. The community would no longer be a possible rupture and a utopia *to come* but rather, through an effort of conscience, an unveiling of the relationship to the Other – human and non-human – that is always already there, awaiting. Not a community as a given fact – as if it were already realised and just waiting to be lived – because it is still an effort, an ongoing work of attentive listening and the action that ensues from this, that of the ruin of the Self in the instant of a relationship to the Other. And yet *immediate* possibility, in each relationship to that which is not myself and whose thread one would only have to grasp to realise that it is perhaps the right one and then, from there, "simply begin".

References

Benjamin Walter, "On the concept of History", 1940, (trans. Dennis Redmond, 2005), https://www.marxists.org/reference/archive/benjamin/1940/history.htm.

Benjamin Walter, "Critique de la violence", in *Œuvres I*, W. Benjamin, Paris, Gallimard, (trans. Maurice de Gandilhac, Rainer Rochlitz and Pierre Rusch), 2000, p. 210–243.

Bensussan Gérard, *Le temps messianique, temps historique et temps vécu*, Paris, Vrin, 2001.

Buber Martin, *The Origin and Meaning of Hassidism*, New York, Horizon Press, 1960.

Buber Martin, *Gog and Magog*, New York, Syracuse University Press, 1999.

Funkenstein Amos, Chalier Catherine, *Maïmonide: Nature, histoire et messianisme*, Paris, Cerf, 2007.

Galanté Avram, "Nouveaux documents sur Sabbataï Zevi", in Galante A., *Histoire des juifs de Turquie*, Istanbul, Isis, 1986, p. 169–292.

Levinas Emmanuel, *Autrement qu'être ou au-delà de l'essence*, Paris, Le Livre de Poche, 2004.

Levinas Emmanuel, *Quatre lectures talmudiques*, Paris, Minuit, 2005.

Maimonides Moses, *Michné Torah, Sefer Shoftim*, no. 12(1), https://www.sefaria.org/Mishneh_Torah%2C_Kings_and_Wars.12?lang=en.

Maimonides Moses, *Commentary on the Michna. Sanhedrin*, https://www.sefaria.org/Rambam_on_Mishnah_Sanhedrin.10.1?lang=en.

Nancy Jean-Luc, *The Inoperative Community*, London, University of Minnesota Press, 2012.

Rosenzweig Franz, Glatzer Nahum Robert, *Franz Rosenzweig: His Life and Thought*, Indianapolis, Hackett, 1998.

Scholem Gershom, "Isaac Luria and his school", in Scholem G., *Major Trends in Jewish Mysticism: Based on the Hilda Strook Lectures Delivered at the Jewish Institute of Religion*, New York, Schocken, 1946, p. 244–286.

Scholem Gershom, *The Messianic Idea in Judaism and Other Essays on Jewish Spirituality*, New York, Schocken, 2011.

Servigne Pablo *et alii* (eds.), *Une autre fin du monde est possible. Vivre l'effondrement (et pas seulement y survivre)*, Paris, Seuil, 2018.

Treaty of Sanhedrin, 98b, https://www.sefaria.org/Sanhedrin.98b?lang=en.

The global context of men's fashion photography in contemporary Russia

Graham Roberts

Introduction

As brands, fashion retailers both reflect the dominant gender ideology in a given society and help circulate that very ideology (Schroeder, Zwick 2004). Yet although much has been written on the politics of women's fashion and fashion imagery in a variety of geographical and historical environments (Bartlett 2010, Tarlo 2010), relatively few scholars have made a serious attempt to place men's fashion imagery in its ideological context. Those that have, have tended to focus on the English-speaking world (Nixon 1996, Jobling 2005, Edwards 2016). Furthermore, they have mostly concentrated on fashion advertising by high-street brands in mainstream publications, thereby restricting themselves to instances where fashion brands have colluded with the dominant ideology rather than critiquing it – two notable recent exceptions are Geczy and Karaminas (2017) and McCauley Bowstead (2018). To gain a better understanding of the kind of social commentary that men's fashion and fashion imagery might engage in, we also need to look outside the mainstream and beyond the Western world.

One place that has seen a number of globally renowned fashion designers emerge in recent years – and that has a well-established tradition of art as social critique – is Russia. The work of designers such as Ul'yana Sergeenko, Tigran Avetisyan and Gosha Rubchinskiy can be seen in articles published online by Russia's growing army of fashion bloggers and also at major international fashion shows (including the annual Mercedes-Benz Fashion Week Russia). There is much that is specifically Russian about these designers. Rubchinskiy in particular has made a number of explicit references in his work to the Russia of his teenage years. His Spring/Summer 2018 show, for example, was staged in the building where raves were first staged in St. Petersburg in the 1990s (Cadogan, Hope Allwood 2017). In an article on "the post-Soviet aesthetic in fashion", Fedorova (n.d.) has suggested that in this and other ways, "the work of Gosha Rubchinskiy turned the experience of growing up in 1990s Russia into a new subculture". As McCauley Bowstead, one of the remarkably small number of academics to have looked at Rubchinskiy, has argued:

> Rubchinskiy's designs of geometrically patterned shell suits; high-waisted sweatpants; satiny shorts and vests, turquoise, lime green, and red colourways; and be-logoed sportswear – along with his use of skinny teenage models – speak of the turbulence of the Perestroika-era Soviet Union and of the period of confusion, desperation, and creativity that accompanied its collapse in the 1990s as Western fashions flooded in (McCauley Bowstead 2018: 159).

McCauley Bowstead is clearly justified in arguing that what he calls the "edginess" (2018: 159) Rubchinskiy brings to contemporary sportswear has its roots in the quite specific historical and political context of 1900s Russia. Be that as it may, it is I believe nevertheless essential to place their work in the broader, global context of contemporary fashion. As Geczy and Karaminas (2017), Bennett (2018), McCauley Bowstead (2018) and others have shown, that context is one in which fashion designers as diverse as Walter van Beirendonck, Marc Jacobs, Charles Jeffrey and Palomo Spain (Fig. 1) are increasingly "queering" gender, and in particular masculinity. This can be seen as an integral part of the "menswear revolution" that as McCauley Bowstead discusses (2018: 123–24) can be traced back, at least in the West, to the mid-to-late 1900s and early 2000s, with designers such as Helmut Lang (for Prada and Miu Miu), Raf Simons (for Jil Sander) and Hedi Slimane (at Yves Saint Laurent and then Dior).

Rather than take us further away from the post-Soviet context, however, the issue of masculinity only serves to bring that context into even sharper relief. Historically, masculinity and the male body have frequently been instrumentalized by the country's political leaders (Kon 2003). Indeed, in recent years Russia and many other ex-Soviet states have been increasingly marked by the politicization of masculinity, and indeed the emergence of hegemonic, heteronormative, homophobic masculinity as a central pillar of national identity (Baer 2009, Sperling 2015, OC Media

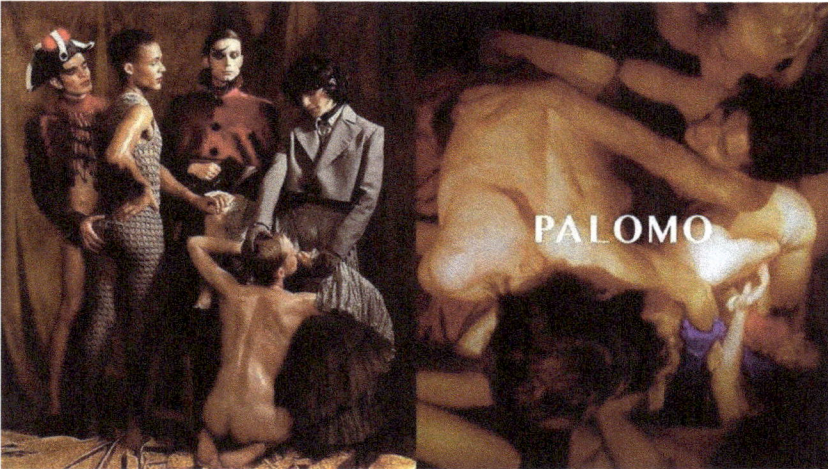

Fig. 1. Palomo Spain's Autumn/Winter 2019 collection, photographed by Matt Lambert (Moss 2019).

2018). In many respects, Russia in particular has become under Vladimir Putin, the land of "extreme masculinity" (Roberts 2017c), a country in which it is becoming increasingly difficult to, in the words of Stella (2012) "carve out [a] queer space". The question is, then: how do Teplov, Gassiline and Rubchinskiy negotiate the artistic, cultural – and indeed ideological – tensions between on the one hand this local, post-Soviet context which shaped them and to which they continue to allude (and to which they are increasingly drawn), and on the other hand the global fashion business in which their images increasingly circulate? How, to put it more succinctly, might their different "fashionscapes" (Karaminas 2012) be said to challenge heteronormative, hegemonic masculinity? My objective in this article is to answer that question.

Serguei Teplov's *Sailor Kiss*

Serguei Teplov is a Russian designer who was born in the Urals (the mountain range separating European and Asian Russia) in the late 1970s. On his official website, he claims (in English) to have "always been different from the people around him" and to have succeeded in creating his own label in spite of the "sorry plight" of the fashion business in Russia

(Telpov n.d.). He also mentions that he has been attending fashion weeks since 2005. The images I discuss are taken from a recent collection of both menswear and womenswear collections, highlighted on his website, and titled *Sailor Kiss* [*sic*] (Telpov n.d.). This collection is presented in a series of eleven monochrome photographs featuring two female models and two male models (all apparently in their early to mid-twenties), represented in a variety of numerical combinations and poses. In some of the photographs, the models are shown standing by the windows of a room that looks out onto the streets of an unidentified city, whereas in others they are standing against a bare wall. They are generally wearing loose-fitting, high-necked, dark clothes (in stark contrast to the overexposed city beyond the window). Although at times the women's clothes leave parts of their bodies exposed (midriff, shoulders, arms, or calves), the men's bodies are covered up; except for one scene, in which one of the men appears to be wearing baggy shorts that extend below his knees, the only parts of their bodies that we can see are their hands (and faces). In two of the scenes, one of the women wears a very different garment, a dress featuring a top covered in horizontal stripes and a bold floral print skirt, over which she wears a jacket of the same striped/floral print. Horizontal stripes (typically blue and white) are of course a prominent feature of the modern uniform of the Russian sailor (and indeed of the *marinière*, an official feature of the French naval uniform since 1858, but more recently "camped up" by French fashion designer Jean-Paul Gaultier). Their hats are also reminiscent of naval dress (although perhaps more twentieth-century United States than twenty-first-century Russia). At the same time, these hats have a distinct Chinese look about them (with their conical shape and upturned brim, they recall the hats worn by officials of the Qing Dynasty in the nineteenth century), as do the rest of the models' garments. This oriental feel is at odds with the location, however; the onion domes of the church one can just about make out in the bleached background of one of the images suggest that we are somewhere in Russia.

Such tensions and ambiguities also extend to the collection's title, *Sailor Kiss*. The stripes (visible in just two of the shots) and the hats aside, there are no visual allusions to sailors. There is no kissing to be seen either. Indeed, one wonders just what the relationship between these various characters is. In some scenes, they barely acknowledge each other. As we contemplate the two youthfully innocent male figures in Fig. 2a, for example, they look neither back at us, nor up, nor off. Instead, they gaze awkwardly inward – toward but crucially past each other. They hold their bodies as awkwardly as that gaze; both figures are rigid, with hands held limply by their sides and legs straight, in a pose as unnatural as it surely must be uncomfortable. They appear trapped within the picture frame, unable to move, not just in the psychological sense of not knowing where to move to but also in the very physical sense of being incapable of movement. At the same time, there is an almost self-consciously androgynous air about these two figures, as suggested by their featureless looks and their physical frames, which are neither muscular nor skinny. The fact that they are shot – "captured" might be a better word – at midshot and at eye level makes it difficult to attribute them with a sex, or indeed to tell whether what the figure on the left is wearing is a pair of shorts or a skirt. This sexual ambivalence is even more apparent in Fig. 2b, where the male character this time verges on the androgynous. Unlike in Fig. 2a, this time he does acknowledge the viewer's gaze. Here too, however, there is no defiant resistance to that gaze; rather, there is an uneasy compliance, an attitude reinforced by the postures of the two women on either side of him, one of whom (the woman on the left) appears to want to protect him, whereas the other (on the right), her arm resting casually on his shoulder, seems a little more willing to let him go.

These images are, as I have already suggested, open to different interpretations. The woman on the left in Fig. 2b, for example, could be saying *You can't have him, he's mine.* In general, however, by the framing, composition, and focal length of the images in this series, the two male characters are constantly marginalized – off to the side, in the background, out of focus – in contrast to their female counterparts, who become the focal point of the shot. Furthermore, the male models in Teplov's *Sailor Kiss* series are potentially feminized by their exposure to the camera, their youthfulness, and their air of passive acquiescence (MacKinnon 1997: 111). Throughout the eleven shots that make up this series, Teplov's female models return the viewer's gaze far more directly and defiantly than the men. Furthermore, this viewer is no longer invited to look narcissistically *with* the male model – as is conventionally the case in men's fashion imagery – but rather longingly and voyeuristically *at* him (MacKinnon 1997: 110). In a sense, of course, this is only to be expected. Teplov's images bear out the point made by Karaminas (2013), echoing Elliott and Elliott (2005), to the effect that much men's fashion photography in effect creates a visual space that invites the heterosexual male viewer to assume more than one subject position at the same time.

Figs. 2a and 2b. Images from Serguei Teplov's *Sailor Kiss* collection
(Teplov n.d.).

Such a viewer may identify with the male model or, rather like heterosexual women or homosexual men, may "*desire* and *consume* the male
image", thereby "indulg[ing] and participat[ing] in homosocial/homo-
erotic behavior in culturally acceptable ways" (Karaminas 2013: 366;
italics in the original). The point, of course – and this is crucial – is that
such behavior is far from "culturally acceptable" in the context of Putin's
Russia. Overall, however, the homoeroticism in Teplov's *Sailor Kiss* is

relatively restrained; the male models' bodies remain more or less covered up and are generally kept at a quite respectable midshot distance, thereby allowing us to see either their entire body or the torso, arms, and face together. It is a quite different matter when it comes to Cyrille Gassiline.

Cyrille Gassiline

Like Teplov, Cyrille Gassiline is a relatively young designer who has acquired a significant following in Russia in recent years. Known for his laconic, at times even minimalist – but nevertheless practical – dresses and shirts, Gassiline undertook an internship in the mid-2000s in the house of Parisian haute couture stylist Dominique Sirop before setting up his own Moscow-based brand in 2008. The images I discuss in the following are from his men's spring and summer 2016 collection, as featured on his official website (Gassiline n.d.).

Visually, these images, which number seventeen in all, share some features with those of Teplov. The men are photographed in stark monochrome inside an unidentified building. Most of the images are midshot. Here is where the visual similarities end between Teplov and Gassiline. Unlike the models in *Sailor Kiss*, Gassiline's are generally photographed alone (in eleven out of the seventeen images); in those rare shots where we see more than one man (there are no women, presumably reflecting the fact that this is a men's collection), there is no acknowledgment of the other's presence, let alone any interaction between them. The tone, too, is a good deal more sombre, both literally – many of the models are framed not by high windows but by dark walls, furniture, and drapes – and figuratively. As for the metaphorical gloom, this is provided by the models themselves. Exuding an air of melancholy, so still as to be almost lifeless, they stare dolefully into the void from behind vacant eyes. These men do not merely appear to be mournful, however; the camera uses a variety of techniques to objectify, and reify, them. In some images, we see only fragments of body parts, such as a pair of deathly pale, prominently veined hands placed dejectedly over a lap. In two of the photographs, the male subject actually resembles an object; he is pictured seating rigidly upright in a chair, naked from the waist up, staring blankly down at the floor and covered with a transparent veil, as if he were a piece of furniture packed away for the winter. There is one shot of the back of a man seen leaning forward on a table in front of an arched window, where living flesh appears to turn into something very different: inanimate (and quite cold) marble (Fig. 3a).

These last two examples – the veil-covered torso and the marble-like back – are remarkable for the way in which the camera eroticizes the

Figs. 3a and 3b. Cyrille Gassiline's men's Spring/Summer 2016 collection (Gassiline n.d.).

male model. This eroticization is accentuated by the high monochrome contrast, which brings out every ripple, every sinew of the models' flesh. There are, of course, other ways to expose oneself than by removing one's clothes. In the final example from Gassiline's spring and summer 2016 collection (Fig. 3b), the male subject lies on his back on a couch or chaise longue, staring vacantly into the air. This kind of exposure leaves him not so much eroticized as feminized. This feminization is both metaphorical (MacKinnion 1997) and literal; if Teplov's male models, with their rigid torsos and dark-colored tunics, call to mind Picasso's *Boy in Blue* (painted in 1905), one can see in Gassiline's supine model a much earlier (feminine) figure: the *Ophelia* of Pre-Raphaelite Sir John Everett Millais, painted between 1851 and 1852 (this may be a conscious decision on Gassiline's part: in the past the designer had worked closely with Russian fashion critic and art historian Aleksandr Vassil'ev).

Although Teplov's and Gassiline's images call to mind iconic images from (Western) art history, Gassiline's images nevertheless eroticize, and indeed sexualize, the male body far more than Teplov's images. This effect is produced in three ways. First, there are the positions adopted by some of Gassiline's men; leaning forward with their backs to us or reclining with their arms by their sides, they appear almost to be inviting the viewer to take advantage of their physical vulnerability. They appear before us in various states of undress, and the lighting effects bring their bodies into sharp relief, whereas Teplov's lighting tends to flatten his models, lending them an almost two-dimensional air. In effect, Gassiline's camera abandons all pretense; unlike in *Sailor Kiss*, the male viewing subject now has no choice but to look at naked male flesh (indeed, at times, this is all we can see). The commodification of the male body is also far greater than in the case of Teplov, for there we generally see the entire body, including the face, although here we often see simply a fragment of that body, in the shape of a body part. Indeed, these images offer a perfect example of the point made by Craik in reference to men's fashion photography in the 1990s West that "the male body has been sexualized by dissection into fetishized objects of desire" (Craik 2004: 199).

Despite the differences in presentation, the fashion photography of Serguei Teplov and Cyrille Gassiline has much in common when it comes to representing the male body. The body is static, exposed, vulnerable, self-conscious, and objectified. As such, the kind of masculinity it represents is anything but heroic. Most importantly, in both collections there is a significant homoerotic element that is profoundly at odds with the hegemonic masculinity that currently enjoys so much currency in Russia. At this point, however, I must introduce a caveat. It is all very well to seek to impose an alternative reading in a sign, but I must nevertheless avoid losing sight of the visual conventions in which that sign emerges and circulates. In other words, the images of the male body that I have examined herein take on a different meaning depending on the visual context or the sign system – what Lotman (1990) calls the "semiosphere" – in which I place them. More precisely, although they may appear to be relatively heterodox in the context of contemporary Russian popular visual culture, it could be argued that they are much more orthodox when placed in the context of men's fashion photography globally. One only has to flick through the pages of Western high-end fashion magazines such as *Vogue Hommes* or *Dazed and Confused* to realize that the array of male body images currently on offer for consumption is very broad indeed, ranging from the "hypermasculine" to the "ultra-thin" (Barry 2014: 289). These images include both the androgynous (in the work of, for example, Christian Dior's designer Hedi Slimane: Rees-Roberts 2013) and the homoerotic (Geczy Karaminas 2016). Furthermore, as van der Laan and Kuipers (2016: 63) have shown, there is a quite specific high-fashion aesthetic, one that photographers and models consciously work to create, in which, as they put it, "actors look for an aesthetic that departs from everyday attractiveness" – and, one might add, anything else resembling the "everyday", including the "norms" governing the performance of gender and sexuality (van der Laan, Kuipers 2016: 63). Crucially, this aesthetic often cuts across national boundaries.

We need to bear in mind, however, that fashion imagery circulates in a variety of different contexts. These include catwalks, glossy magazines, e-stores, lookbooks, and digital film (Needham 2013, Rees-Roberts 2018). And although each of these visual formats may now be available globally, in the digital age, it is important not to overlook the fact that they often emerge in quite specific, not to say highly political, local contexts. At times, those specific contexts may emerge quite explicitly, not to say self-consciously. In order to appreciate this, one need look no further than Gosha Rubchinskiy, to whom I shall now turn.

Gosha Rubchinskiy

A graduate of the Moscow State University of Design and Technology, Rubchinskiy first made his name as a fashion photographer and designer of street wear, before being signed up by Adrian Joffe at Comme des Garçons in 2012. His brand, wholly owned by Comme des Garçons, currently occupies a 270-foot square space in the basement of the new Dover Street Market on London's Haymarket, near Piccadilly Circus (although Rubchinskiy himself is still based in Russia, and his last three shows to date have been staged in that country). Writing on fashion at the very end of the twentieth century, Evans contends that the recent information and technological revolution had transformed the fashion image from "mere representation" to "the commodity itself" (Evans 2013: 86). Rubchinskiy's work stands as eloquent testimony to Evans' argument. In a Russian-language interview published in 2013, he went as far as to claim that the main reason he chose to pursue a career in fashion was not the clothes themselves, but rather that working in this area "would enable me to express myself, through photography, through video, through various things" (The Village 2013). Commenting on his first ever show (given in Moscow in 2008), Rubchinskiy has claimed: "It was not about the collection, but about these boys, this generation, this energy" (Kansara, Fedorova 2016). Adrian Joffe sees him not "as a fashion designer, but as a photographer, a recorder of things" (Kansara, Fedorova 2016).

Rubchinskiy's interest in visually recording not just any "things", but the quite specific, and at times extreme, masculinity of teenage boys in particular may be why in 2016 he helped design the *Mad About The Boy* exhibition, curated by Lou Stoppard at SHOWstudio, a fashion film website. This exhibition, as Stoppard herself has put it, "explored fashion obsession with youth, focusing on the way ideas of the teen boy are constructed through specific collections and images" (SHOWstudio n.d.). His photo albums, his videos, and his catwalks, are full of Russian teenage boys, many of whom idolize him (Madsen 2017). These boys, and the masculinity they embody, are central to his creative activity. Indeed, if Dostoevsky once claimed that "beauty will save the world", Rubchinskiy openly enlists what he refers to as the "beauty" of his models in an attempt to challenge the negative image of Russia generated by Western media as part of what he has called an "informational [sic] war" against his native country (YouTube 2015). This increasingly involves "queering" masculinity, by inviting a homoerotic gaze.

As I have argued elsewhere (Roberts 2017b), questioning (not to say "queering") accepted, Western notions of masculine "beauty" often appears more important to Rubchinskiy than designing fashion. One of the first examples of this tendency in his fashion imagery (as distinct from his non-fashion videos such as *Transformation*, 2012) can be found in his Spring/Summer 2015 lookbook. The model here is notable for the skinny arms poking out of his t-shirt, his self-consciously gauche air, his physical vulnerability (an effect only amplified by his sitting with legs apart), and his crudely, garishly painted fingernails (Fig. 4).

The shaved head that features here and began to emerge in Rubchinskiy's fashion photography around the time of his Spring/Summer 2015 lookbook has now established itself as a central pillar of the designer's "look" (this is not, however, to suggest that *all* his runway models have shaved heads). It is, I would like to argue, an essential part of Rubchinskiy's "queering" of masculinity (on the homoeroticism of the shaven headed model in Rubchinskiy's Spring/Summer 2016 lookbook, see

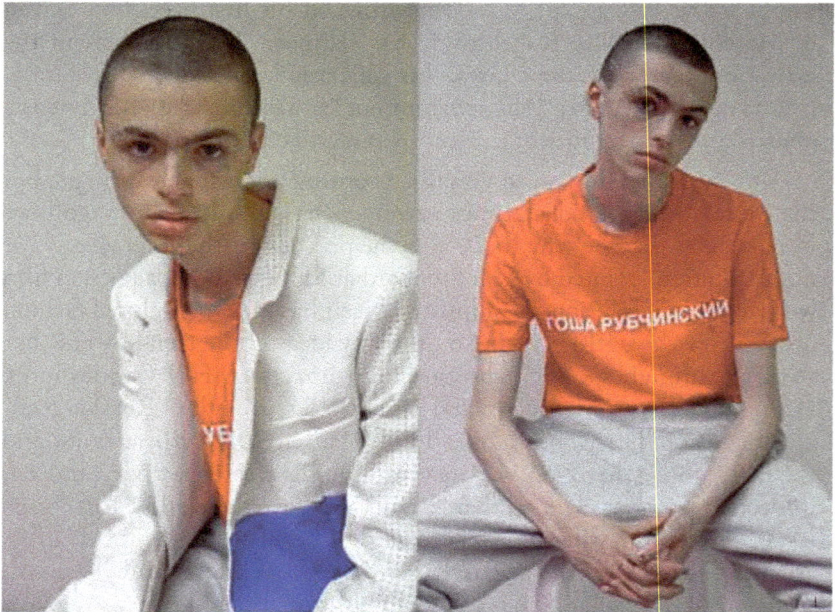

Fig. 4. The male model from Rubchinskiy's Spring/Summer 2015 lookbook (Rubchinskiy n.d.).

Roberts 2017a). It was during his 2016 Pitti Uomo show, staged in a disused cigarette factory on the outskirts of Florence, that the fashion press first began to notice it, and see it as a distinctive feature of Rubchinskiy's visual style. As one commentator put it, at Pitti Uomo Rubchinskiy "cast a crew of Soviet-looking teenage boys with bleached buzz cuts and without facial hair as the models. They were a sharp contrast to the usual Pitti peacocks" (Petrarca 2016). The shaved heads of many of his models, combined with their youthfulness and inexperience, and the clothes they wore – such details certainly helped them stand out in Florence. More importantly, they suggested unbridled, (not to say criminalized) male sexuality of the kind personified in and explored by the dedicatee of the show, Pier Paolo Pasolini. Indeed, as Muret (2016) puts it, referring specifically to Pasolini's work: "Wearing sneakers, retro tracksuits and loose sweatshirts and chains on their necks, they were reminiscent of Pier Pasolini's [novel] *Ragazzi di vita* [1955], the rent boys plying their trade in Rome's suburbs described by the Italian poet, writer and director, who inspired the Russian designer for his Spring/Summer 2017 collection". This look, this body image, has led Katerina Zolototrubova, fashion editor of Russian *Vogue*, to compare Rubchinskiy's models to the "gopniki", a Russian-language term meaning "bad boys from the suburbs" (Ferrier 2016).

Rubchinskiy's predilection for the shaven-headed "gopnik" look was particularly prominent during his Autumn/Winter 2017 show, staged in the Russian city of Kaliningrad (formerly Prussian Königsberg) in January 2017. This show signaled a return to Russia for Rubchinskiy, and as such it held particular personal significance for the designer, who in an interview compared it explicitly to his "Empire of Evil" show held in Moscow in 2008 (Kansara 2017). Whereas Rubchinskiy's show in 2008 featured elements – including bears and Kalashnikovs – specifically designed to parody western views of Russia and Russian masculinity through caricature, his January 2017 show was on the contrary intended to be far less provocative. The image of masculinity that Rubchinskiy displayed in Kaliningrad is very much a hybrid – in the same way that much of the clothing on display involved a collaboration between Rubchinskiy and the western sports brand Adidas. While a number of models sported the shaved heads, purposeful gazes and angular chins characteristic of Rubchinskiy's Pitti Uomo "gang" members (Fig. 5), the acne-ridden cheeks and self-conscious postures of a number of his models – at least one of whom was as young as 16 - suggested a very different kind of boyish innocence, not to say vulnerability.

The collective result was described by one critic as a "poetic new masculinity" (Madsen 2017: 172: for a short video of the show, which includes footage of one particular model having his hair shaved in preparation for the show, see In Russia 2017).

Shaven-headed models were a prominent feature of this show, and indeed of his two subsequent shows, the first in June 2018, in a location in St. Petersburg famous for hosting the city's first post-Soviet raves, and

Fig. 5. A model from Rubchinskiy's Autumn/Winter 2017 show, Kaliningrad (Madsen 2017).

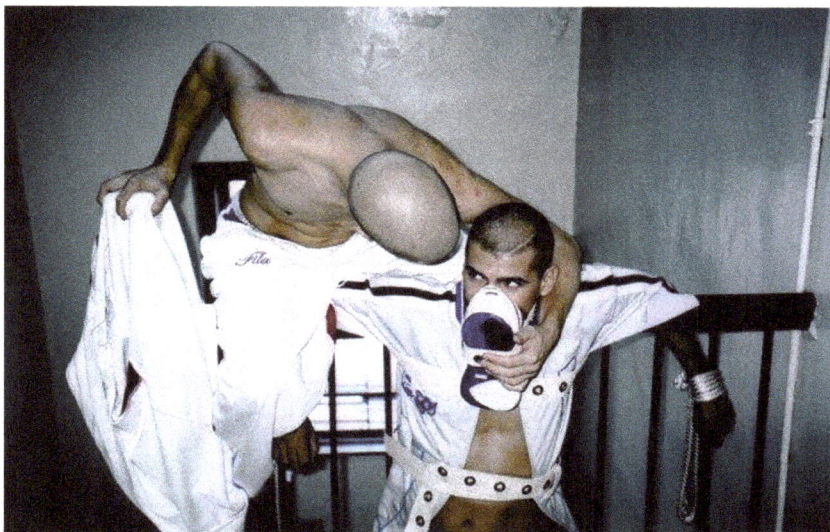

Fig. 6. "Sneaker Sniffer (Josh and Herbert), New York City 2003" (from Mogutin's series "No Love", 2004) (Mogutin n.d.).

the second in the Urals city of Yekaterinburg in early 2019 – the last to date (December 2018). In an interview given as part of a documentary video for *i-D*, one of Rubchinskiy's stylists claims: "We like shaved heads, because [that way] nothing distracts from a person's face" (i-D 2017). It may well have its practical advantages; one of the most significant points about the skinheaded "gopnik" look, however, is that – in Rubchinskiy's work at least – it acquires deeply homoerotic overtones. As such, it is part of what I would argue is a conscious attempt on his part to "queer" conventional, heteronormative notions of masculinity. As anthropologist Hilary Pilkington has observed, in an article on skinheads in northern Russia: "The skinhead body has undergone a profound eroticization for the outside gaze through the photographs of Slava Mogutin, the subgenre of 'skinhead' films within gay porn, and the appropriation of its visual style as the ultimate sexual fantasy in gay circles" (Pilkington 2010: 188; for an example of Mogutin's homoerotic representation of the young male skinhead, see Fig. 6).

Conclusion

In her keynote address at the recent End of Fashion Conference in Wellington, New Zealand, Valerie Steele suggested that "fashion is not just about clothes; it is also about new ways of seeing and thinking" (Steele 2016). Evans (2013), on the other hand, suggests that where both fashion and fashion imagery are concerned, there is precious little that is genuinely "new". Evans's point is borne out by the images I have been discussing here. Destabilizing the male gaze, and the rigid binaries of gender and sexuality on which that gaze is premised, the photographs featured on the websites of Serguei Teplov, Cyrille Gassiline, and Gosha Rubchinskiy reach across space as well as time. Visually, and indeed ideologically, they are remarkably reminiscent of the imagery of contemporary Western designers such as Walter van Beirendonck, Marc Jacobs, Charles Jeffrey and Palomo Spain, whom we mentioned in our introduction. In this important sense, they are inevitably at odds with the kind of masculinity that enjoys hegemony in their local Russian context. In this crucial sense, they suggest that the notion of heteronormative male power on which that hegemonic masculinity rests is nothing but another mythical, ideological construct, to paraphrase Geczy and Karaminas (2017: 2). In the final analysis, these images suggest that fashion photography, especially men's fashion photography, remains a space where representation is still "fascinating, powerful, and dangerous", to quote Still (2003: 4). How long it continues to enjoy that privileged position in Putin's Russia remains to be seen.

References

Baer Brian James, *Other Russias: Homosexuality and the Crisis of Post-Soviet Identity*, Basingstoke, Palgrave Macmillan, 2009.

Barry Ben, "Expanding The Male Ideal: The Need for Diversity in Men's Fashion Advertisements", in *Critical Studies in Men's Fashion*, no. 1(3), 2014, p. 275–293.

Bartlett Djurdja, *FashionEast: The Spectre that Haunted Socialism*, Cambridge (MA) and London, The MIT Press, 2010.

Bennett Parker, "Menswear in the Millennium: Bending the Gender Binary", in Lynch A., Medvedev K. (eds.), *Fashion, Agency and*

Empowerment: Performing Agency, Following Script, London and New York, Bloomsbury, 2018, p. 63–81.

Cadogan Dominic, Hope Allwood Emma, "Gosha's SS18 Show: Russian Rave and a New Zine", in *Dazed*, 10 June 2017, http://www.dazeddigital.com/fashion/article/36280/1/gosha-rubchinskiy-ss18-show-burberry-russia-rave-zine-adidas.

Craik Jeniffer, *The Face of Fashion: Cultural Studies in Fashion*, London and New York, Routledge, 2004.

Edwards Tim, *Men in the Mirror: Men's Fashion, Masculinity and Consumer Society*, London and New York, Bloomsbury, 2016.

Elliott Richard, Elliott Christine, "Idealized Images of the Male Body in Advertising: A Reader-Response Exploration", in *Journal of Marketing Communications*, no. 11(1), 2005, p. 3–19.

Evans Caroline, "Yesterday's Emblems and Tomorrow's Commodities: The Return of the Repressed in Fashion Imagery Today", in Bruzzi S., Church Gibson P. (eds.), *Fashion Cultures Revisited*, Abingdon and New York, Routledge, 2013, p. 77–102.

Fedorova Anastasiia, "The Post-Soviet Aesthetic", in *The Calvert Journal*, [n.d.], http://www.calvertjournal.com/features/show/8070/post-soviet-aesthetic-fashion-trend-ltfr-belinskiy-yefimtchuk-bevza.

Ferrier Morwenna, "The Man Who Made Russian Fashion Cool", in *The Guardian*, 12 October 2016, https://www.theguardian.com/fashion/2016/oct/12/russian-fashion-gosha-rubchinskiy-post-soviet-designer-menswear.

Gassiline Cyrille, http://cyrille.gassiline.com/.

Geczy Adam, Karaminas Vicki, *Fashion's Double: Representations of Fashion in Painting, Photography and Film*, London, Bloomsbury, 2016.

Geczy Adam, Karaminas Vicki, *Critical Fashion Practice: From Westwood to Van Beirendonck*, London and New York, Bloomsbury, 2017.

i-D, "Inside Gosha Rubchinskiy's Post-soviet Generation", 31 July 2017, https://www.youtube.com/watch?v=zZLVXgHxqVI&t=196s.

In Russia, "Apart. Gosha Rubchinskiy's Show in Kaliningrad", 5 March 2017, https://www.youtube.com/watch?v=dBicm6PFAN0.

Jobling Paul, *Man Appeal: Advertising, Modernism and Men's Wear*, Oxford, Berg, 2005.

Kansara Vikram Alexei, Fedorova Anastasiia, "How Comme des Garçons Grew Gosha Rubchinskiy", *Business of Fashion*, 17 March 2016, https://www.businessoffashion.com/articles/bof-exclusive/comme-des-garcons-gosha-rubchinskiy-dover-street-market-london.

Kansara Vikram Alexei, "How Gosha Rubchinskiy and Adidas Are Refashioning Football", in *Business of Fashion*, 12 January 2017, https://www.businessoffashion.com/articles/bof-exclusive/gosha-rubchinskiy-adidas-kaliningrad-globalization-localization.

Karaminas Vicki, "Image: Fashionscapes. Notes Toward an Understanding of Media Technologies and Their Impact on Contemporary Fashion Imagery", in Geczy A., Karaminas V. (eds.), *Fashion and Art*, London and New York, Berg, 2012, p. 177–187.

Karaminas Vicki, "Vampire Dandies: Fashionable Masculine Identities and Style in Popular Culture", in Bruzzi S., Church Gibson P. (eds.), *Fashion Cultures Revisited: Theories, Explorations and Analysis*, Abingdon and New York, Routledge, 2013, p. 366–376.

Kon Igor, *Muzhskoe telo v istorii kul'tury*, Moscow, Slovo, 2003.

Lotman Yury, *Universe of the Mind. A Semiotic Theory of Culture*, London and New York, I. B. Tauris, 1990.

MacKinnon Kenneth, *Uneasy Pleasures: The Male as Erotic Object*, London, Cygnus Arts, 1997.

Madsen Anders Christian, "From Russia with Love: We Meet Gosha Rubchinskiy and His Gang", i-D, 27 March 2017, https://i-d.vice.com/en_uk/article/j5mxwp/from-russia-with-love-we-meet-gosha-rubchinskiy-and-his-gang.

McCauley Bowstead Jay, *Menswear Revolution: The Transformation of Contemporary Men's Fashion*, London and New York, Bloomsbury, 2018.

Mogutin Slava [n.d.], "No Love", http://slavamogutin.com/no-love/.

Moss Jack, "Palomo Spain's Latest Campaign is a Sensual Celebration of Queer Romance", in *Another Man*, 22 July 2019, https://www.anothermanmag.com/style-grooming/10901/palomo-spains-latest-campaign-is-a-sensual-celebration-of-queer-romance.

Muret Dominique, "Gosha Rubchinskiy Takes His Bad Boys' Gang to Pitti Uomo", *Fashion Network*, 16 June 2016, http://se.fashionnetwork.com/news/Gosha-Rubchinskiy-takes-his-bad-boys-gang-to-Pitti-Uomo,704123.html#.WNi-4mU02b9.

Needham Gary, "The Digital Fashion Film", in Bruzzi S., Church Gibson P. (eds.), *Fashion Cultures Revisited. Theories, Explorations and Analysis*, Abingdon and New York, Routledge, 2013, p. 103–111.

Nixon Sean, *Hard Looks: Masculinities, Spectatorship and Contemporary Consumption*, London, Routledge, 1996.

OC Media, "Queer Rights Activists Cancel Tbilisi 17 May Demonstration After 'Threats From Far-Right Groups'", 16 May 2018, http://oc-media.org/queer-rights-activists-cancel-17-may-demonstration-after-threats-from-far-right-groups/.

Office, "Gosha Rubchinskiy SS 18", 14 June 2017, http://officemagazine.net/gosha-rubchinskiy-ss18.

Petrarca Emilia, "Gosha's Gang: A Who's Who of the Designer's Inner Circle", in *W*, 15 June 2016, https://www.wmagazine.com/gallery/gosha-rubchinskiy-spring-2017-pitti-uomo/all.

Rees-Roberts Nick, "Boys Keep Swinging: The Fashion Iconography of Hedi Slimane", in *Fashion Theory: The Journal of Dress, Body and Culture*, no. 17(1), 2013, p. 7–26.

Rees-Roberts Nick, *Fashion Film: Art and Advertising in the Digital Age*, London, Bloomsbury, 2018.

Roberts Graham H., "Homo Post-sovieticus: (Re)fashioning the Male Body in the New Russia", in *Journal of Asia-Pacific Pop Culture*, no. 2(1), 2017a, p. 6–29.

Roberts Graham H., "Leader of the Gang: Gosha Rubchinskiy and the Death of the Catwalk", in *Fashion Theory: The Journal of Dress, Body and Culture*, no. 21(6), 2017b, p. 689–707.

Roberts Graham H., "Angels With Dirty Faces: Gosha Rubchinskiy and the Politics of Style", in *Journal of Extreme Anthropology*, no. 1(3), 2017c, p. 18–40, https://www.journals.uio.no/index.php/JEA/article/view/5564/4941.

Rubchinskiy Gosha, "Spring/Summer 2015 Lookbook", http://gosharubchinskiy.com/collection/ss2015/.

Schroeder Jonathan E., Zwick Detlev, "Mirrors of Masculinity: Representation and Identity in Advertising Images", in *Consumption, Markets and Culture*, no. 7(2), 2004, p. 21–52.

SHOWstudio, "Mad About The Boy", http://showstudio.com/project/mad_about_the_boy, n.d.

Sperling Valerie, *Sex, Politics and Putin*, Oxford and New York, Oxford University Press, 2015.

Steele Valerie, *A Queer History of Fashion: From the Closet to the Catwalk*, New Haven and London, Yale University Press/The Fashion Institute of Technology, 2013.

Steele Valerie, "Keynote Lecture", paper presented at the "End of Fashion" conference, Wellington, New Zealand, 8–9 December 2016.

Stella Francesca, "The Politics of In/Visibility: Carving Out Queer Space in Ul'yanovsk", in *Europe-Asia Studies*, no. 64(10), 2012, p. 1822–1846.

Still Judith, "(Re)presenting Masculinities: Introduction to *Men's Bodies*", in Still J. (ed.), *Men's Bodies*, Edinburgh, Edinburgh University Press, 2004, p. 1–14.

Tarlo Emma, *Visibly Muslim: Fashion, Politics, Faith*, London, Bloomsbury, 2010.

Teplov Serguei, www.sergueiteplov.com.

The Village, "Gosha Rubchinskiy i Alisher: Chto tvoritsya v rossiiskoi mode?", 11 September 2013, https://www.the-village.ru/village/city/teatalks/131529-fashion.

Van der Laan Elise, Kuipers Giselinde, "Creating Aesthetic, Institutional and Symbolic Boundaries in Fashion Photo Shoots", in *International Journal of Fashion Studies*, no. 3(1), 2016, p. 47–68.

YouTube, "Gosha Rubchinskiy. In Fashion Interview, Uncut Footage", 26 October 2015, https://www.youtube.com/watch?v=EFW4y5Iyh_Q.

Series Published Titles

Vol. 19   Anna Louyest et Graham Roberts (éds)
           Etre russe, écrire à l'étranger. 2013
           ISBN 978-3-0343-1113-7

Vol. 20   Stephanie Rohlfing-Dijoux et Kerstin Peglow (éds)
           *La subsidiarité. Regards croisés franco-allemands sur un principe
           pluridisciplinaire.* 2013
           ISBN 978-3-0343-1135-9

Vol. 21   Pascale Cohen-Avenel (éd.)
           *Jazz, pouvoir et subversion de 1919 à nos jours / Jazz, Macht und Subversion
           von 1919 bis heute.* 2014
           ISBN 978-3-0343-1414-5

Vol. 22   Bernd Zielinski, Jean-Robert Raviot (éds.)
           *Les élites en question. Trajectoires, réseaux et enjeux de gouvernance :
           France, UE, Russie.* 2014
           ISBN 978-3-0343-1413-8

Vol. 23   Valérie de Daran & Marion George (éds)
           *Eclats d'Autriche. Vingt études sur l'image de la culture autrichienne aux
           XXe et XXIe siècles.* 2014
           ISBN 978-3-0343-1477-0

Vol. 24   Brigitte Krulic (dir.)
           *Savoirs et métiers de l'Etat au XIXe siècle. France et Etats
           germaniques.* 2014
           ISBN 978-3-0343-1504-3

Vol. 25   Dorothée Cailleux, Serguei Sakhno et Jean-Robert Raviot (dir.)
           Situations de plurilinguisme et politiques du multilinguisme en Europe.
           2016
           ISBN 978-2-87574-353-4

Vol. 26   François Morvan
           Aux sources de l'esprit français : la liberté de traduire. 2017
           ISBN 978-2-8076-0544-2

Vol. 27   Florence Xiangyun Zhang et Keling Wei (dir.)
           *Recherche et traduction
           Une vision engagée de la traduction.* 2018
           ISBN 978-3-0343-1504-3

Vol. 28   Sophie Guermès et Brigitte Krulic (dir.)
           Edgar Quinet, une conscience européenne. 2018
           ISBN 978-2-8076-0632-6

Vol. 29   Christine Bouneau & Laurent Coste (dir.)
           Les conseillers du pouvoir en Europe du XVIᵉ siècle à nos jours.
           Acteurs, cercles et pratiques. 2018
           ISBN 978-2-8076-0833-7

Vol. 30   Adrien Frenay, Giulio Iacoli et Lucia Quaquarelli (dir.)
           Traverser. Mobilité spatiale, espace, déplacements. 2019
           ISBN 978-2-8076-0679-1

Vol. 31   Hervé Bismuth, Fritz Taubert (eds.)
           Le Serment / Der Eid. De l'âge du Prince à l'ère des nations /
           Vom Zeitalter der Fürsten bis zur Ära der Nationen. 2020
           ISBN 978-2-8076-1581-6

Vol. 34   Florence Xiangyun Zhang et Nicolas Froeliger (dir.)
           Traduire, un engagement politique
           ISBN 978-2-8076-1716-2

Vol. 35   Pascale Cohen-Avenel, Lucia Quaquarelli (eds.)
           Thinking in Common. Community in the Global Era
           ISBN 978-2-8076-1412-3

www.peterlang.com

www.ingramcontent.com/pod-product-compliance
Lightning Source LLC
Chambersburg PA
CBHW052012270326
41929CB00015B/2885